taste of home.
GROUND BEEF

CASSEROLES • SOUPS • STOVETOP • SLOW COOKER & MORE!

13

70   51

100   103

23

34

101

19

90

contents

on the cover
Photographer Grace Natoli Sheldon
Food Stylist Shannon Roum
Set Styling Manager Stephanie Marchese

Pictured on front cover:
Pizza Tot Casserole, page 60

Pictured on back cover:
Cheeseburger Paradise Soup, page 18

Crowd-Pleasing Taco Salad, page 107

Chipotle Sliders, page 12

60

taste of home · Reader's Digest

EDITORIAL
Editor-in-Chief Catherine Cassidy

Executive Editor/Print & Digital Books Stephen C. George
Creative Director Howard Greenberg
Editorial Services Manager Kerri Balliet

Senior Editor/Print & Digital Books Mark Hagen
Editor Christine Rukavena
Associate Creative Director Edwin Robles Jr.
Art Director Raeann Sundholm
Content Production Manager Julie Wagner
Layout Designer Nancy Novak
Copy Chief Deb Warlaumont Mulvey
Copy Editor Alysse Gear
Contributing Copy Editor Valerie Phillips

Recipe Editor Mary King
Recipe Content Manager Colleen King
Assistant Photo Coordinator Mary Ann Koebernik
Recipe Testing Taste of Home Test Kitchen
Food Photography Taste of Home Photo Studio
Editorial Assistant Marilyn Iczkowski

BUSINESS
Vice President, Publisher Jan Studin, jan_studin@rd.com
Regional Account Director Donna Lindskog,
donna_lindskog@rd.com
Eastern Account Director Joanne Carrara
Eastern Account Manager Kari Nestor
Account Manager Gina Minerbi
Midwest & Western Account Director Jackie Fallon
Midwest Account Manager Lorna Phillips
Michigan Sales Representative Linda C. Donaldson
Southwestern Account Representative Summer Nilsson

Corporate Digital & Integrated Sales Director, N.A. Steve Sottile
Associate Marketing Director, Integrated Solutions Katie Gaon Wilson
Digital Sales Planner Tim Baarda

General Manager, Taste of Home Cooking Schools Erin Puariea

Direct Response Advertising Katherine Zito, David Geller Associates

Executive Director, Brand Marketing Leah West
Senior Marketing Manager Vanessa Bailey
Associate Marketing Manager Betsy Connors

Vice President, Magazine Marketing Dave Fiegel

READER'S DIGEST NORTH AMERICA
Vice President, Business Development Jonathan Bigham
President, Books and Home Entertaining Harold Clarke
Chief Financial Officer Howard Halligan
Vice President, General Manager,
Reader's Digest Media Marilynn Jacobs
Chief Marketing Officer Renee Jordan
Vice President, Chief Sales Officer Mark Josephson
General Manager, Milwaukee Frank Quigley
Vice President, Chief Content Officer Liz Vaccariello

THE READER'S DIGEST ASSOCIATION, INC.
President and Chief Executive Officer Robert E. Guth

© 2013 Reiman Media Group, Inc.
5400 S. 60th St. Greendale, WI 53129

International Standard Book Number: 978-1-61765-171-7
Library of Congress Control Number: 2012913122

Ground Beef... A Dinnertime Lifesaver

CATHERINE CASSIDY
EDITOR-IN-CHIEF

When it comes to setting a hot meal on the table, ground beef always fits the bill! Fast, easy and economical, this dinner staple just can't be beat! After all, nothing satisfies hungry appetites like a bubbling casserole, cheesy lasagna or piping-hot chili, all made hearty with ground beef.

You'll always have dozens of dinner options on hand with *Taste of Home Ground Beef*! Flip through our pages of flavorful favorites and you'll find more than 200 recipes and tips, guaranteed to make meals a snap and keep your family asking for more.

Inside, you'll discover over 4 dozen simple **Stovetop Suppers**. Choose from classics such as Best Spaghetti and Meatballs (p. 41) and Zesty Tacos (p. 36), or enjoy a new flavor sensation with tasty choices like Hawaiian Beef (p. 58) and Greek-Style Ravioli (p. 40). Each is table-ready in just 25 minutes!

The aroma of hearty meat loaves, golden potpies and more will warm your home when you bake up a recipe from **Casseroles & Oven Entrees**. No one can resist Salisbury Steak with Gravy (p. 87) and fun Cheeseburger Pockets (p. 61). With this tempting chapter, choosing what to make first will be your biggest challenge!

No ground beef cookbook would be complete without hot-off-the-grill burgers, crowd-pleasing sloppy joes and other satisfying **Sandwiches**. Meat lovers of all ages will revel in finger-licking Meatball Subs (p. 28) and Smothered Onion Patty Melts (p. 32).

You'll also find dozens of **Soups, Stews and Chili** recipes, as well as **Slow Cooker** specialties that cut kitchen time. Turn to the **Appetizers & Munchies** chapter for irresistible stromboli, pizzas and nacho plates that promise to tame hunger in the tastiest ways. They're ideal snacks or light meals, and they make entertaining a breeze!

Finally, round out your meal with hot side dishes, stuffed breads and other savory choices from **Sides & More**. You'll be the star at your next potluck, family reunion or church supper with Western-Style Beef and Beans (p. 100), crispy Crowd-Pleasing Taco Salad (p. 107) or any other must-try recipe in this chapter.

Whether you need a fast dinner, a special way to complete a menu or an appetizer for the big game, turn to *Taste of Home Ground Beef* for surefire results your family won't soon forget.

Enjoy!

Catherine

"This recipe has to be the ultimate in a fast-fixing mini burger with simply fabulous flavor! Creamy mayo, cheese and sweet Hawaiian rolls help tame the heat of the chipotle peppers."

— **SHAWN SINGLETON** VIDOR, TEXAS
about his recipe, Chipotle Sliders, on page 12

6

13

14

Appetizers & Munchies

Mini Burgers with the Works

PREP/TOTAL TIME: 30 MIN.
MAKES: 1 DOZEN

- ¼ pound ground beef
- 3 slices process American cheese
- 4 slices white bread (heels of loaf recommended)
- 2 tablespoons prepared Thousand Island salad dressing
- 2 pearl onions, thinly sliced
- 4 baby dill pickles, thinly sliced
- 3 cherry tomatoes, thinly sliced

1. Shape beef into twelve 1-in. patties. Place on a microwave-safe plate lined with paper towels. Cover with another paper towel; microwave on high for 1 minute until meat is no longer pink.
2. Cut each slice of cheese into fourths; set aside. Using a 1-in. round cookie cutter, cut out six circles from each slice of bread.
3. Spread half of the bread circles with dressing. Layer with burgers, cheese, onions, pickles and tomatoes.
4. Top with remaining bread circles; secure with toothpicks.

Editor's Note: *This recipe was tested in a 1,100-watt microwave.*

Cheese Meatballs

I often rely on these rich, cheesy meatballs for easy party appetizers. You can also serve them alongside a tossed salad with fresh warm bread for a satisfying meal that's ready in minutes.

— RACHEL FROST TALLULA, ILLINOIS

PREP: 20 MIN. **BAKE:** 15 MIN.
MAKES: ABOUT 4 DOZEN

- 3 cups (12 ounces) finely shredded cheddar cheese
- 1 cup biscuit/baking mix
- ½ teaspoon salt
- ¼ teaspoon pepper
- ¼ teaspoon garlic powder
- 1 pound lean ground beef (90% lean)

1. In a large bowl, combine the cheese, biscuit mix, salt, pepper and garlic powder. Crumble ground beef over the mixture and mix well.
2. Shape into 1-in. balls. Place meatballs on a greased rack in a shallow baking pan.
3. Bake at 400° for 12-15 minutes or until the meat is no longer pink; drain.

I started preparing these mini burgers several years ago as a way to use up bread crusts. Their tiny size makes them simply irresistible.

— LINDA LANE BENNINGTON, VERMONT

MINI BURGERS WITH THE WORKS

Southwestern Bean Dip

Just by using different types of beans, you can make this dip as spicy as you like it. My family could eat this as their entire meal.

— **JEANNE SHEAR** SABETHA, KANSAS

PREP: 20 MIN. **BAKE:** 30 MIN.
MAKES: ABOUT 9 CUPS

- 2 **pounds ground beef**
- 1 **tablespoon dried minced onion**
- 1 **can (8 ounces) tomato sauce**
- 1 **can (16 ounces) kidney beans, rinsed and drained**
- 1 **can (16 ounces) chili beans, undrained**
- 4 **cups (16 ounces) shredded cheddar cheese**
    Tortilla chips

1. In a large skillet, cook beef over medium heat until no longer pink; drain. Transfer to a bowl; add onion. Set aside.
2. In a blender, process tomato sauce and beans until chunky. Add to beef mixture and mix well. Spoon half into a greased 13-in. x 9-in. baking dish; top with half of the cheese. Repeat layers.
3. Bake, uncovered, at 350° for 30 minutes or until cheese is melted. Serve warm with chips.

Snack Rye Toasts

With the irresistible combination of creamy cheese and lightly seasoned meat on crispy toast, these snacks get cleared away quickly.

— **CAROLYN SNOW** SEDALIA, MISSOURI

PREP/TOTAL TIME: 30 MIN.
MAKES: 3 DOZEN

- 1 **pound ground beef**
- 1 **pound bulk Italian sausage**
- 1 **pound process cheese (Velveeta), cubed**
- 3 **tablespoons Worcestershire sauce**
- 3 **tablespoons ketchup**
- 1 **teaspoon garlic salt**
- 1 **teaspoon dried oregano**
- ¼ **teaspoon salt**
- ¼ **teaspoon pepper**
- 1 **loaf (1 pound) snack rye bread**

1. In a large skillet over medium heat, cook beef and sausage until no longer pink; drain. Add the cheese, Worcestershire sauce, ketchup and seasonings; stir until cheese is melted. Spread 1 to 2 tablespoons hot mixture on each bread slice. Place on ungreased baking sheets.
2. Freeze pizzas or bake at 350° for 10-15 minutes or until heated through.

To use frozen toasts: *Bake at 350° for 15- 20 minutes or until heated through.*

Pepperoni Stromboli

I've made this delicious stromboli many times. It's perfect when friends and family get together to watch football and basketball games. It always satisfies big appetites.

— **SHELLEY BANZHAF** MAYWOOD, NEBRASKA

PREP: 25 MIN. + RISING **BAKE:** 30 MIN. **MAKES:** 2 LOAVES (8 SERVINGS EACH)

- 2 **loaves (1 pound each) frozen bread dough, thawed**
- 2 **eggs, lightly beaten**
- ⅓ **cup olive oil**
- ½ **teaspoon each garlic powder, salt and pepper**
- ½ **teaspoon ground mustard**
- ½ **teaspoon dried oregano**
- 1 **pound ground beef, cooked and drained**
- 1 **package (3½ ounces) sliced pepperoni**
- 2 **cups (8 ounces) shredded part-skim mozzarella cheese**
- 1 **cup (4 ounces) shredded cheddar cheese**
- 1 **small onion, chopped**

1. Place each loaf of bread dough in a greased large bowl, turning once to grease top. Cover and let rise in a warm place until doubled, about 45 minutes. Punch down. Roll each loaf into a 15-in. x 12-in. rectangle.
2. In a small bowl, combine the eggs, oil and seasonings. Brush over dough to within ½ in. of edges; set remaining egg mixture aside. Layer beef, pepperoni, cheeses and onion on dough to within ½ in. of edges. Roll up, jelly-roll style, beginning with a long side. Seal the edges well.
3. Place seam side down on greased baking sheets. Brush with remaining egg mixture. Bake at 375° for 30-35 minutes or until lightly browned. Let stand for 5-10 minutes before cutting.

top tip For an appetizer buffet that serves as a meal, offer five or six different appetizers (including some substantial selections) and plan on eight to nine pieces per guest. If you'll also be serving a meal, two to three pieces per person is sufficient. Look for appetizers that can be made ahead and require little last-minute fuss so you can visit more with guests.

Barbecue Beef Taco Plates

I prepared this hearty appetizer for 200 people at a cookout, and it was gone before I knew it! Everyone loved the combination of barbecued ground beef, veggies and cheese.

— **IOLA EGLE** BELLA VISTA, ARKANSAS

PREP: 20 MIN. **COOK:** 20 MIN.
MAKES: 2 PLATES (20 SERVINGS EACH)

- 4 pounds ground beef
- 2 envelopes taco seasoning
- 1 cup water
- 4 packages (8 ounces each) cream cheese, softened
- 1 cup 2% milk
- 2 envelopes ranch salad dressing mix
- 4 cans (4 ounces each) chopped green chilies, drained
- 1 cup chopped green onions
- 3 to 4 cups shredded romaine
- 2 cups (8 ounces) shredded cheddar cheese
- 4 medium tomatoes, seeded and chopped
- 2 to 3 cups honey barbecue sauce
- 2 to 3 packages (13½ ounces each) tortilla chips

1. In a Dutch oven, cook beef over medium heat until no longer pink; drain. Stir in taco seasoning and water. Bring to a boil. Reduce heat; simmer, uncovered, for 15 minutes.
2. In a large bowl, beat the cream cheese, milk and dressing mixes until blended. Spread over two 14-in. plates. Layer with the beef mixture, chilies, onions, romaine, cheese and tomatoes. Drizzle with barbecue sauce.
3. Arrange some tortilla chips around the edge; serve with remaining chips.

Meatball Calzones

PREP: 1½ HOURS + STANDING **BAKE:** 25 MIN.
MAKES: 3 CALZONES (4 SERVINGS EACH)

- 3 eggs, lightly beaten
- 1 cup seasoned bread crumbs
- 1 cup grated Parmesan cheese
- 3 teaspoons Italian seasoning
- 2 pounds ground beef
- 3 loaves (1 pound each) frozen bread dough, thawed
- 3 cups (12 ounces) shredded part-skim mozzarella cheese
- 1 egg white, lightly beaten
  Additional Italian seasoning
- 1 jar (14 ounces) spaghetti sauce, warmed

1. In a large bowl, combine the eggs, bread crumbs, Parmesan cheese and Italian seasoning. Crumble beef over mixture and mix well. Shape into 1-in. balls.
2. Place meatballs on a rack in a shallow baking pan. Bake, uncovered, at 400° for 10-15 minutes or until no longer pink. Drain on paper towels. Reduce heat to 350°.
3. On a floured surface, roll each portion of dough into an 18-in. x 12-in. rectangle. Spoon a third of the meatballs and mozzarella cheese down the center of each rectangle. Fold dough over filling; press edges firmly to seal.
4. Place on greased baking sheets. Brush tops with egg white; sprinkle with Italian seasoning. Let stand for 15-30 minutes. Bake for 25-30 minutes or until golden brown. Serve with spaghetti sauce.

> ❝My family can't get enough of these fun calzones. We have to have them at least once a month, or everyone goes through withdrawal. Leftovers freeze well for a quick snack later. ❞

— **CORI COOPER** BOISE, IDAHO

Picante Egg Rolls

Living near the Mexican border, we've developed a passion for spicy cuisine. I came up with this recipe by mixing and matching some foods we already craved.

— **MARILYN LONG** SPRING VALLEY, CALIFORNIA

PREP: 20 MIN. **COOK:** 5 MIN./BATCH
MAKES: 2½ DOZEN (1½ CUPS SAUCE)

- 2 pounds ground beef
- 2 cups (8 ounces) shredded cheddar cheese
- ½ cup picante sauce
- 1 envelope chili seasoning
- 1 teaspoon garlic powder
- 2 packages (16 ounces each) egg roll wrappers
  Oil for deep frying

SAUCE
- 1 cup picante sauce
- ½ cup sour cream

1. In a large skillet, cook beef over medium heat until no longer pink; drain. Remove from the heat. Stir in the cheese, picante sauce, chili seasoning and garlic powder.

2. Place ¼ cupful in the center of an egg roll wrapper. (Keep remaining wrappers covered with a damp paper towel until ready to use.) Fold bottom corner over filling. Fold sides toward center over filling. Moisten remaining corner with water; roll up tightly to seal. Repeat.

3. In an electric skillet or deep fryer, heat oil to 375°. Fry egg rolls, a few at a time, for 2-3 minutes on each side or until golden brown. Drain on paper towels. Combine sauce ingredients; serve with egg rolls.

Bacon Cheeseburger Pizza

Kids of all ages love pizza and cheeseburgers, and this recipe combines them. My grandchildren usually request pizza for supper when they visit me. They like to help me make this version, and they especially enjoy eating it!

— **CHERIE ACKERMAN** LAKELAND, MINNESOTA

PREP/TOTAL TIME: 20 MIN. **MAKES:** 8 SLICES

- ½ pound ground beef
- 1 small onion, chopped
- 1 prebaked 12-inch pizza crust
- 1 can (8 ounces) pizza sauce
- 6 bacon strips, cooked and crumbled
- 20 dill pickle coin slices
- 2 cups (8 ounces) shredded part-skim mozzarella cheese
- 2 cups (8 ounces) shredded cheddar cheese
- 1 teaspoon pizza or Italian seasoning

1. Cook beef and onion in a large skillet over medium heat until meat is no longer pink; drain and set aside.

2. Place crust on an ungreased 12-in. pizza pan. Spread with pizza sauce. Top with beef mixture, bacon, pickles and cheeses. Sprinkle with pizza seasoning. Bake at 450° for 8-10 minutes or until cheese is melted.

Party Meatballs

These meatballs in a sweet, tangy sauce can be made a day in advance and reheated. They are terrific for big family gatherings.

— **IRMA SCHNUELLE** MANITOWOC, WISCONSIN

PREP: 40 MIN. **BAKE:** 15 MIN. **MAKES:** ABOUT 5 DOZEN

- ¾ cup evaporated milk
- 1 envelope onion soup mix
- 5 teaspoons Worcestershire sauce, divided
- 2 pounds ground beef
- 2 cups ketchup
- 1 cup packed brown sugar

1. In a large bowl, combine the milk, soup mix and 2 teaspoons Worcestershire sauce. Crumble beef over mixture and mix well.

2. With wet hands, shape mixture into 1-in. balls. Place meatballs on a greased rack in a shallow baking pan. Bake, uncovered, at 400° for 12 minutes or until meat is no longer pink. Drain on paper towels.

3. Meanwhile, combine the ketchup, brown sugar and remaining Worcestershire sauce in a Dutch oven. Bring to a boil over medium heat. Cook and stir until thickened. Reduce heat; add meatballs. Simmer until heated through, about 15 minutes.

Enchilada Meatballs

PREP: 20 MIN. **BAKE:** 20 MIN.
MAKES: ABOUT 4½ DOZEN

- 2 cups crumbled corn bread
- 1 can (10 ounces) enchilada sauce, divided
- ½ teaspoon salt
- 1½ pounds ground beef
- 1 can (8 ounces) tomato sauce
- ½ cup shredded Mexican cheese blend

1. In a large bowl, combine the corn bread, ½ cup enchilada sauce and salt. Crumble beef over mixture; mix well. Shape into 1-in. balls.

2. Place meatballs on a greased rack in a shallow baking pan. Bake, uncovered, at 350° for 18-22 minutes or until meat is no longer pink; drain.

3. Meanwhile, in a small saucepan, heat tomato sauce and remaining enchilada sauce. Drain meatballs; place in a serving dish. Top with sauce and sprinkle with cheese. Serve with toothpicks.

Mini Oven Burgers

My hearty snacks are perfect for Sunday afternoon football games and teen parties. For the mini buns, I use pan dinner rolls. This is an easy way to make lots of yummy appetizers to feed a crowd.

— **JUDY LEWIS** STERLING HEIGHTS, MICHIGAN

PREP: 15 MIN. **BAKE:** 25 MIN.
MAKES: 40 SERVINGS

- ½ cup chopped onion
- 1 tablespoon butter
- 1 egg, lightly beaten
- ¼ teaspoon seasoned salt
- ¼ teaspoon ground sage
- ¼ teaspoon salt
- ⅛ teaspoon pepper
- 1 pound lean ground beef (90% lean) or ground beef
- 40 mini buns, split
- 8 ounces process American cheese slices, cut into 1½-inch squares, optional
- 40 dill pickle slices, optional

1. In a large skillet, saute onion in butter. Transfer to large bowl; add egg and seasonings. Crumble beef over mixture and mix well. Spread over bottom halves of the buns; replace tops. Place on baking sheets; cover with foil.

2. Bake at 350° for 20 minutes or until meat is no longer pink. If desired, place a cheese square and pickle on each hamburger; replace tops and foil and return to the oven for 5 minutes.

Before I retired, I'd often bring these tasty little treats to share at work. They're a good way to use up leftover corn bread.

— **MEARL HARRIS** WEST PLAINS, MISSOURI

ENCHILADA MEATBALLS

Pigs in a Blanket

Here's an awesome update to classic pigs in a blanket. A yummy mixture of pork and beef gets wrapped up in from-scratch pastry dough. Bet you can't eat just one!

— **CYNDI FYNAARDT** OSKALOOSA, IOWA

PREP: 45 MIN. **BAKE:** 35 MIN.
MAKES: ABOUT 4½ DOZEN

- 3 cups all-purpose flour
- 1 tablespoon sugar
- 2 teaspoons baking powder
- ½ cup shortening
- ½ cup cold butter
- 1 cup milk
- 10 crushed Zwieback or Holland rusks (1¼ cups)
- ¼ teaspoon salt
- ¼ teaspoon pepper
- 1¾ pounds ground beef
- 1¾ pounds bulk pork sausage
  Dijon mustard, optional

1. In a large bowl, combine the flour, sugar and baking powder. Cut in shortening and butter until mixture resembles coarse crumbs. Gradually add milk, tossing with a fork until dough forms a ball. Divide dough into three portions. Refrigerate until chilled.

2. Meanwhile, for filling, in a large bowl, combine the Zwieback crumbs, salt and pepper. Crumble beef and pork over mixture and mix well. Shape rounded tablespoonfuls of meat mixture into 3-in. logs; set aside.

3. On a floured surface, knead one portion of dough 8-10 times. Roll dough to ⅛-in. thickness; cut with a floured 3-in. round cutter.

4. Place one log in the center of each circle. Brush edges of dough with water; fold dough over filling and pinch edges to seal. Reroll scraps. Repeat with remaining dough and filling.

5. Place on greased racks in shallow baking pans. Bake at 350° for 35-40 minutes or until a thermometer reads 160°. Serve with mustard if desired.

Pizza Fondue

PREP/TOTAL TIME: 25 MIN. **MAKES:** 5½ CUPS

- ½ pound ground beef
- 1 cup chopped fresh mushrooms
- 1 medium onion, chopped
- 1 garlic clove, minced
- 1 tablespoon cornstarch
- 1½ teaspoons fennel seed
- 1½ teaspoons dried oregano
- ¼ teaspoon garlic powder
- 2 cans (15 ounces each) pizza sauce
- 2½ cups (10 ounces) shredded cheddar cheese
- 1 cup (4 ounces) shredded part-skim mozzarella cheese
- 2 tablespoons chopped ripe olives
  Breadsticks, bagel chips, baked pita chips and/or tortilla chips

1. In a large skillet, cook the beef, mushrooms and onion over medium heat until meat is no longer pink. Add garlic; cook 1 minute longer. Drain. Stir in the cornstarch, fennel, oregano and garlic powder until blended. Stir in pizza sauce.

2. Bring to a boil; cook and stir for 1-2 minutes or until thickened. Gradually stir in cheeses until melted. Stir in olives. Keep warm.

3. Serve with breadsticks, bagel chips, pita chips and/or tortilla chips.

❝ Great for a party or game-day gathering, this satisfying dip can be made with Italian sausage instead of ground beef if you prefer. Add a little more pizza sauce if it seems too thick. ❞

— **MARGARET SCHISSLER** MILWAUKEE, WISCONSIN

Chipotle Sliders

This recipe has to be the ultimate in a fast-fixing mini burger with simply fabulous flavor! Creamy mayo, cheese and sweet Hawaiian rolls help tame the heat of the chipotle peppers.

— **SHAWN SINGLETON** VIDOR, TEXAS

PREP/TOTAL TIME: 30 MIN.   **MAKES:** 10 SLIDERS

- 1 package (12 ounces) Hawaiian sweet rolls, divided
- 1 teaspoon salt
- ½ teaspoon pepper
- 8 teaspoons minced chipotle peppers in adobo sauce, divided
- 1½ pounds ground beef
- 10 slices pepper jack cheese
- ½ cup mayonnaise

1. Place 2 rolls in a food processor; process until crumbly. Transfer to a large bowl; add the salt, pepper and 6 teaspoons chipotle peppers. Crumble beef over mixture and mix well. Shape into 10 patties.

2. Grill burgers, covered, over medium heat for 3-4 minutes on each side or until a thermometer reads 160° and juices run clear. Top with cheese. Grill 1 minute longer or until cheese is melted.

3. Split remaining rolls and grill, cut side down, over medium heat for 30-60 seconds or until toasted. Combine mayonnaise and remaining chipotle peppers; spread over roll bottoms. Top each with a burger. Replace roll tops.

Freezer Burritos

I love burritos, but the frozen ones are so high in salt and processed ingredients. So I created these. They're great to have on hand for quick dinners or late-night snacks—even breakfast!

— **LAURA WINEMILLER** DELTA, PENNSYLVANIA

PREP: 35 MIN.   **COOK:** 15 MIN.   **MAKES:** 12 SERVINGS

- 1¼ pounds lean ground beef (90% lean)
- ¼ cup finely chopped onion
- 1¼ cups salsa
- 2 tablespoons reduced-sodium taco seasoning
- 2 cans (15 ounces each) pinto beans, rinsed and drained
- ½ cup water
- 2 cups (8 ounces) shredded reduced-fat cheddar cheese
- 12 flour tortillas (8 inches), warmed

1. In a large skillet, cook beef and onion over medium heat until meat is no longer pink; drain. Stir in salsa and taco seasoning. Bring to a boil. Reduce heat; simmer, uncovered, for 2-3 minutes. Transfer to a large bowl; set aside.

2. In a food processor, combine the pinto beans and water. Cover and process until almost smooth. Add to beef mixture. Stir in cheese.

3. Spoon ½ cup beef mixture down the center of each tortilla. Fold ends and sides over filling; roll up. Wrap each burrito in waxed paper and foil. Freeze for up to 1 month.

To use frozen burritos: *Remove foil and waxed paper. Place one burrito on a microwave-safe plate. Microwave on high for 2½ to 2¾ minutes or until a thermometer reads 165°, turning burrito over once. Let stand for 20 seconds.*

Editor's Note: *This recipe was tested in a 1,100-watt microwave.*

Sloppy Joe Nachos

When my kids were little, they adored these snacks they could eat with their fingers. It makes a great quick meal, tailgate food or treat when you have the munchies.

— **JANET RHODEN** HORTONVILLE, WISCONSIN

PREP/TOTAL TIME: 15 MIN.   **MAKES:** 6 SERVINGS

- 1 pound ground beef
- 1 can (15½ ounces) sloppy joe sauce
- 1 package (12 ounces) tortilla chips
- ¾ cup shredded cheddar cheese
- ¼ cup sliced ripe olives, optional

1. In a large skillet, cook beef over medium heat until no longer pink; drain. Add sloppy joe sauce; cook, uncovered, for 5 minutes or until heated through.

2. Arrange tortilla chips on a serving plate. Top with meat mixture, cheese and olives if desired.

A nifty cross between wontons and tacos, these triangles are fun to serve. My mom created the recipe years ago, much to the delight of my family. Since I began making them, my husband insists we have them on Sundays during football season as well as for holidays.

— **SHELIA POPE** PRESTON, IDAHO

SOUTHWEST WONTONS

Southwest Wontons

PREP: 25 MIN. + COOLING **COOK:** 40 MIN.
MAKES: ABOUT 7½ DOZEN

- 1 **pound ground beef**
- 1 **medium onion, chopped**
  Salt and pepper to taste
- 1 **can (16 ounces) refried beans**
- 1½ **cups (6 ounces) shredded cheddar cheese**
- 1 **cup salsa**
- 1 **can (4 ounces) diced jalapeno peppers, drained**
- 2 **packages (12 ounces each) wonton wrappers**
  Oil for deep frying
  Additional salsa

1. In a large skillet over medium heat, cook the beef, onion, salt and pepper until meat is no longer pink; drain. Add the beans, cheese, salsa and jalapenos. Cook and stir over low heat until the cheese is melted. Remove from the heat; cool for 10 minutes.

2. Place a teaspoonful of beef mixture in the center of one wonton wrapper. Moisten edges with water. (Keep remaining wrappers covered with a damp paper towel until ready to use.) Fold wonton in half, forming a triangle; press edges to seal. Repeat.

3. In an electric skillet or deep fryer, heat oil to 375°. Fry wontons, a few at a time, for 2-3 minutes or until golden brown. Drain on paper towels. Serve warm with additional salsa.

Kid-Size Pizzas

The ingredients for this recipe can always be found in my kitchen for snacks or last-minute meals. Our two young boys like to personalize their pizzas with different toppings.

— **RACHEL DEVAULT** GROVE CITY, OHIO

PREP/TOTAL TIME: 25 MIN.
MAKES: 12 SERVINGS

- 1 **package (12 ounces) English muffins, split and toasted**
- 1 **jar (14 ounces) pizza sauce**
- 1 **pound ground beef, cooked and drained**
- 2 **cups (8 ounces) shredded part-skim mozzarella cheese**

Place muffins on an ungreased baking sheet. Spread with pizza sauce. Sprinkle with the beef and cheese. Bake at 425° for 5 minutes or until cheese is melted.

Zesty Nacho Dip

PREP/TOTAL TIME: 30 MIN.
MAKES: 8 CUPS

- 2 **pounds ground beef**
- 2 **pounds process cheese (Velveeta), cubed**
- 1 **can (14½ ounces) stewed tomatoes, cut up**
- 2 **cans (4 ounces each) chopped green chilies**
- 3 **teaspoons chili powder**
- 3 **teaspoons Worcestershire sauce**
  Tortilla chips

1. In a Dutch oven, cook beef over medium heat until no longer pink; drain. Add the cheese, tomatoes, chilies, chili powder and Worcestershire sauce.
2. Cook, uncovered, for 15 minutes or until cheese is melted, stirring occasionally. Serve warm with chips.

Taco Pizzas

Convenient prebaked crust makes this tasty taco pizza as easy as can be. I keep the ingredients on hand so that we can whip up this filling meal anytime.

— **MARY CASS** BALTIMORE, MARYLAND

PREP: 30 MIN. **BAKE:** 10 MIN.
MAKES: 2 PIZZAS (6-8 SLICES EACH)

- 1 **pound ground beef**
- 1 **envelope taco seasoning**
- 1 **cup water**
- 2 **prebaked 12-inch pizza crusts**
- 1 **can (16 ounces) refried beans**
- ¾ **cup salsa**
- 2 **cups coarsely crushed tortilla chips**
- 2 **cups (8 ounces) shredded cheddar cheese**
  Chopped tomatoes and shredded lettuce, optional

1. In a large saucepan, cook beef over medium heat until no longer pink; drain. Stir in taco seasoning and water. Bring to a boil. Reduce heat; simmer, uncovered, for 10 minutes to allow the flavors to blend. Set aside.
2. Place crusts on ungreased pizza pans or baking sheets. Combine beans and salsa; spread over crusts. Top with beef mixture, chips and cheese.
3. Bake at 350° for 13-16 minutes or until cheese is melted. Sprinkle with tomatoes and lettuce if desired.

To increase the zip in this hearty dip, use another can of chilies and Mexican-style stewed tomatoes and processed cheese. You can keep it warm in a slow cooker or fondue pot for easy serving. It's tasty served over baked potatoes, too.

— **DENISE HILL** OTTAWA LAKE, MICHIGAN

ZESTY NACHO DIP

18

17

23

Soups, Stews & Chili

Schoolhouse Chili

PREP: 10 MIN. **COOK:** 70 MIN.
MAKES: 6 SERVINGS

- 1 can (14½ ounces) diced tomatoes, undrained
- 1 can (16 ounces) mild chili beans, undrained
- ½ cup chopped onion
- ¼ cup chopped green pepper
- 1 pound ground beef
- 1½ teaspoons salt
- 1 to 2 teaspoons chili powder
- 1 teaspoon ground cumin
- ½ teaspoon pepper
  Hot cooked spaghetti, optional

1. In a blender, combine the tomatoes, beans, onion and green pepper; cover and puree until smooth.

2. In a large saucepan, cook beef over medium heat until no longer pink; drain. Add seasonings and pureed vegetables. Bring to a boil. Reduce heat; cover and simmer for 1 hour. Serve with spaghetti if desired.

Hominy Meatball Stew

My stew is tasty served with crackers as well as corn bread. For a milder version, use plain canned tomatoes instead of Mexican.

— **DIANE TENNISON** LAFAYETTE, LOUISIANA

PREP: 30 MIN. **COOK:** 45 MIN.
MAKES: 8 SERVINGS (2½ QUARTS)

- 1 egg, lightly beaten
- ½ cup cornmeal
- ¼ cup finely chopped onion
- ½ teaspoon salt
- ⅛ teaspoon pepper
- 1 pound ground beef
- 2 tablespoons canola oil
- 2 cans (15½ ounces each) hominy, rinsed and drained
- 2 cans (14½ ounces each) Mexican diced tomatoes, undrained
- 2 cans (8 ounces each) tomato sauce
- 2 cups water
- 1 envelope taco seasoning

1. In a large bowl, combine the egg, cornmeal, onion, salt and pepper. Crumble beef over mixture and mix well. Shape into ¾-in. balls.

2. In a large skillet over medium heat, brown meatballs in oil in batches. Drain.

3. In a Dutch oven, bring hominy, tomatoes, tomato sauce, water and taco seasoning. Reduce heat; add meatballs. Cover and cook 30 minutes or until no longer pink.

When I was a school cook, the students loved my chili because they thought it didn't have beans in it. They didn't know I puree the beans, tomatoes, onions and green pepper to create a tasty and nutritious dish!

— **MARY SELNER** GREEN BAY, WISCONSIN

SCHOOLHOUSE CHILI

Lasagna Soup

Here's a recipe that's excellent for working mothers because it's fast to make and very flavorful. No one will guess you started with a boxed mix!

— **GLADYS SHAFFER** ELMA, WASHINGTON

PREP: 10 MIN. **COOK:** 30 MIN.
MAKES: 10 SERVINGS (2½ QUARTS)

- 1 **pound ground beef**
- ½ **cup chopped onion**
- 1 **package (7¾ ounces) lasagna dinner mix**
- 5 **cups water**
- 1 **can (14½ ounces) diced tomatoes, undrained**
- 1 **can (7 ounces) whole kernel corn, undrained**
- 2 **tablespoons grated Parmesan cheese**
- 1 **small zucchini, chopped**

1. In a Dutch oven, cook beef and onion over medium heat until meat is no longer pink; drain. Add contents of the lasagna dinner sauce mix, water, tomatoes, corn and cheese; bring to a boil. Reduce heat; cover and simmer for 10 minutes, stirring occasionally.

2. Add the lasagna noodles and zucchini. Cover and simmer for 10 minutes or until noodles are tender.

Hunter's Stew

Since receiving this recipe from a friend years ago, I have appreciated its meal-in-one convenience. While it bakes, I can concentrate on other things I enjoy doing.

— **ANNE REYNOLDS** SPRAKERS, NEW YORK

PREP: 20 MIN. **BAKE:** 2 HOURS
MAKES: 4 SERVINGS

- 1 **pound lean ground beef (90% lean)**
- 1 **medium onion, chopped**
- 3 **medium carrots, sliced**
- 3 **large potatoes, peeled and sliced**
- 1 **package (9 ounces) frozen cut green beans, thawed**
- 1 **can (10¾ ounces) condensed tomato soup, undiluted**
- 1⅓ **cups water**

1. Crumble beef into a greased 13-in. x 9-in. baking dish. Layer with the onion, carrots, potatoes and beans. Combine soup and water; pour over beans.

2. Cover and bake at 375° for 2 hours or until the meat is no longer pink and vegetables are tender.

Taco Soup

Popular and easy, Taco Soup offers a bright assortment of colors and flavors. Garnish each serving with shredded cheese, sour cream or sliced jalapenos if you like.

— **JENNIFER VILLARREAL** TEXAS CITY, TEXAS

PREP/TOTAL TIME: 30 MIN. **MAKES:** 8 SERVINGS (ABOUT 2 QUARTS)

- 1½ **pounds ground beef**
- 1 **envelope taco seasoning**
- 2 **cans (15¼ ounces each) whole kernel corn, undrained**
- 2 **cans (15 ounces each) Ranch Style beans (pinto beans in seasoned tomato sauce)**
- 2 **cans (14½ ounces each) diced tomatoes, undrained**
  Crushed tortilla chips and shredded cheddar cheese

In a Dutch oven, cook beef over medium heat until no longer pink; drain. Stir in the taco seasoning, corn, beans and tomatoes. Cover and cook for 15 minutes or until heated through, stirring occasionally. Place tortilla chips in soup bowls; ladle soup over top. Sprinkle with cheese.

top tip When you have time, brown and drain several pounds of ground beef. Spread on a cookie sheet and freeze. Transfer to freezer bags. On busy days, pull out a bag and add to any recipe that uses browned ground beef.
—**KATHY S.** PITTSBURGH, PENNSYLVANIA

Cheeseburger Paradise Soup

I've never met a person who didn't enjoy this creamy soup. It's hearty enough to serve as a main course with your favorite bread or rolls.

— **NADINA IADIMARCO** BURTON, OHIO

PREP: 30 MIN. **COOK:** 25 MIN.
MAKES: 14 SERVINGS (ABOUT 3½ QUARTS)

- 6 medium potatoes, peeled and cubed
- 1 small carrot, grated
- 1 small onion, chopped
- ½ cup chopped green pepper
- 2 tablespoons chopped seeded jalapeno pepper
- 3 cups water
- 2 tablespoons plus 2 teaspoons beef bouillon granules
- 2 garlic cloves, minced
- ⅛ teaspoon pepper
- 2 pounds ground beef
- ½ pound sliced fresh mushrooms
- 2 tablespoons butter
- 5 cups 2% milk, divided
- 6 tablespoons all-purpose flour
- 1 package (16 ounces) process cheese (Velveeta), cubed
  Crumbled cooked bacon

1. In a Dutch oven, bring the first nine ingredients to a boil. Reduce heat; cover and simmer for 10-15 minutes or until potatoes are tender.

2. Meanwhile, in a large skillet, cook beef and mushrooms in butter over medium heat until meat is no longer pink; drain. Add to soup. Stir in 4 cups milk; heat through.

3. In a small bowl, combine flour and remaining milk until smooth; gradually stir into soup. Bring to a boil; cook and stir for 2 minutes or until thickened. Reduce heat; stir in cheese until melted. Garnish with bacon.

Editor's Note: *Wear disposable gloves when cutting hot peppers; the oils can burn skin. Avoid touching your face.*

Texas Ranch-Style Stew

PREP: 10 MIN. **COOK:** 25 MIN. **MAKES:** 6 SERVINGS

- 1 cup small shell pasta
- 1 pound lean ground beef (90% lean)
- 1 medium onion, chopped
- 1 medium green pepper, chopped
- 2 garlic cloves, minced
- 3 cans (5½ ounces each) reduced-sodium V8 juice
- 1 can (15 ounces) Ranch Style beans (pinto beans in seasoned tomato sauce)
- 1 can (14½ ounces) Southwestern diced tomatoes, undrained
- ½ cup frozen corn
- 1 tablespoon chili powder
- ½ teaspoon salt
- ¼ teaspoon pepper

1. Cook pasta according to package directions.

2. Meanwhile, in a large nonstick skillet, cook the beef, onion, green pepper and garlic over medium heat until meat is no longer pink; drain. Stir in the remaining ingredients. Bring to a boil. Reduce heat; simmer, uncovered, for 10 minutes, stirring occasionally. Drain pasta; stir into stew.

“Ground beef, beans and pasta create a satisfying stew that's perfect for brisk autumn days. The zesty, well-seasoned broth gives it an unmistakable Western flair.”

— **SUE WEST** ALVORD, TEXAS

BEEF BARLEY SOUP

Beef Barley Soup

I came across this recipe years ago at a recipe exchange through a church group. The contributor didn't sign her name, so I don't know who to thank. But my husband and son thank me for preparing it by helping themselves to seconds and thirds!

— **ELLEN MCCLEARY** SCOTLAND, ONTARIO

PREP: 10 MIN. **COOK:** 1 HOUR
MAKES: 12 SERVINGS (3 QUARTS)

- 1½ **pounds ground beef**
- 3 **celery ribs, sliced**
- 1 **medium onion, chopped**
- 3 **cans (10½ ounces each) condensed beef consomme, undiluted**
- 1 **can (28 ounces) diced tomatoes, undrained**
- 4 **medium carrots, sliced**
- 2 **cups water**
- 1 **can (10¾ ounces) condensed tomato soup, undiluted**
- ½ **cup medium pearl barley**
- 1 **bay leaf**

In a Dutch oven, cook the beef, celery and onion over medium heat until meat is no longer pink; drain. Add the remaining ingredients; bring to a boil. Reduce heat; simmer, uncovered, for 45-50 minutes or until barley is tender. Discard bay leaf.

Burger Stew

My grandmother gave me this recipe, so it always brings back warm memories of her whenever I prepare it.

— **JULIE KRETCHMAN**
MEYERSDALE, PENNSYLVANIA

PREP: 10 MIN. **COOK:** 55 MIN.
MAKES: 2 SERVINGS

- ½ **pound ground beef**
- ¼ **cup chopped onion**
- ¼ **cup chopped celery**
- 1 **cup canned diced tomatoes, undrained**
- ¾ **cup beef broth**
- ¾ **cup cubed peeled potato**
- ¼ **cup thinly sliced carrot**
- 2 **tablespoons uncooked long grain rice**
- ½ **teaspoon salt, optional**
- ⅛ **teaspoon pepper**

In a large saucepan, cook the beef, onion and celery over medium heat until meat is no longer pink; drain. Stir in the tomatoes, broth, potato, carrot, rice, salt if desired and pepper. Bring to a boil. Reduce heat; cover and simmer 40-45 minutes or until rice and vegetables are tender.

ABC Soup

PREP/TOTAL TIME: 30 MIN.
MAKES: 11 SERVINGS (2¾ QUARTS)

- 1 **pound ground beef**
- 1 **medium onion, chopped**
- 2 **quarts tomato juice**
- 1 **can (15 ounces) mixed vegetables, undrained**
- 1 **cup water**
- 2 **beef bouillon cubes**
- 1 **cup uncooked alphabet pasta**
  Salt and pepper to taste

In a large saucepan, cook beef and onion over medium heat until the meat is no longer pink; drain. Add tomato juice, vegetables, water and bouillon; bring to a boil. Add pasta. Cook, uncovered, for 6-8 minutes or until pasta is tender, stirring frequently. Add salt and pepper.

Editor's Note: *If you don't have small pasta on hand for ABC Soup, use quick-cooking barley or instant rice. Cook until tender. If you're out of bouillon cubes, 2 teaspoons of bouillon granules can be used instead.*

Hamburger Minestrone

Any kind of convenient frozen mixed vegetables and any petite pasta give our special minestrone a special touch of you!

— **TASTE OF HOME TEST KITCHEN**

PREP/TOTAL TIME: 30 MIN.
MAKES: 6 SERVINGS

- ½ **cup uncooked small pasta shells**
- 1 **pound ground beef**
- ½ **cup chopped onion**
- 3 **cans (14½ ounces each) beef broth**
- 1 **package (16 ounces) frozen mixed vegetables**
- 1 **can (16 ounces) kidney beans, rinsed and drained**
- 1 **can (14½ ounces) diced tomatoes, undrained**
- 1 **can (6 ounces) tomato paste**
- 3 **teaspoons Italian seasoning**
- 1 **teaspoon salt**
- ¼ **teaspoon dried thyme**
- ¼ **teaspoon dried basil**
- ¼ **teaspoon pepper**

1. Cook pasta according to package directions. Meanwhile, in a large saucepan, cook beef and onion over medium heat until meat is no longer pink; drain.

2. Stir in the remaining ingredients. Bring to a boil. Reduce heat; simmer, uncovered, for 15 minutes. Drain pasta and add to the pan; heat through.

ABC SOUP

Instead of opening a can of alphabet soup, why not make it from scratch? Kids of all ages love this traditional soup with its tomato base, ground beef and alphabet pasta.

— **SHARON BROCKMAN** APPLETON, WISCONSIN

Flavorful Southwestern Chili

This treasured recipe comes from my grandmother. The chili is full of flavor, freezes beautifully and makes a complete last-minute meal. I adorn it with grated cheddar cheese and chopped black olives and serve tortilla chips on the side.

— **JENNY GREEAR**
HUNTINGTON, WEST VIRGINIA

PREP/TOTAL TIME: 30 MIN.
MAKES: 10 SERVINGS (2½ QUARTS)

- 2 pounds lean ground beef (90% lean)
- 1½ cups chopped onions
- 2 cans (14½ ounces each) diced tomatoes, undrained
- 1 can (15 ounces) pinto beans, rinsed and drained
- 1 can (15 ounces) tomato sauce
- 1 package (10 ounces) frozen corn, thawed
- 1 cup salsa
- ¾ cup water
- 1 can (4 ounces) chopped green chilies
- 1 teaspoon ground cumin
- ½ teaspoon garlic powder

1. In a Dutch oven, cook beef and onions over medium heat until meat is no longer pink; drain. Stir in the remaining ingredients. Bring to a boil. Reduce heat; simmer, uncovered, for 15 minutes.

2. Serve desired amount. Cool the remaining chili; transfer to freezer containers. May be frozen for up to 3 months.

To use frozen chili: *Thaw in the refrigerator. Place in a saucepan; heat through.*

Italian Wedding Soup

After one taste, you'll find that this soup is absolutely delicious. Lean ground beef and reduced-sodium broth help keep it light. For variety, substitute garbanzo beans for the kidney beans.

— **PAULA SULLIVAN** BARKER, NEW YORK

PREP: 35 MIN. **COOK:** 20 MIN. **MAKES:** 7 SERVINGS

- 1 egg, lightly beaten
- 1 tablespoon dry bread crumbs
- 1 tablespoon dried parsley flakes
- 1 tablespoon plus ¼ cup grated Parmesan cheese, divided
- ½ teaspoon onion powder
- ½ teaspoon salt, divided
- ⅛ teaspoon plus ¼ teaspoon pepper, divided
- ½ pound lean ground beef (90% lean)
- ¼ cup uncooked orzo or acini di pepe pasta
- 1 medium onion, finely chopped
- 3 celery ribs, chopped
- 1 tablespoon olive oil
- 2 garlic cloves, minced
- 4 cans (14½ ounces each) reduced-sodium chicken broth
- 1 can (16 ounces) kidney beans, rinsed and drained
- 4 cups chopped fresh spinach

1. In a large bowl, combine the egg, bread crumbs, parsley, 1 tablespoon Parmesan cheese, onion powder, ¼ teaspoon salt and ⅛ teaspoon pepper. Crumble beef over mixture and mix well. Shape into ¾-in. meatballs.

2. Place in a 15-in. x 10-in. x 1-in. baking pan coated with cooking spray. Bake at 350° for 8-10 minutes or until no longer pink; drain.

3. Cook pasta according to package directions; drain. In a large saucepan, saute onion and celery in oil until tender. Add garlic; cook 1 minute longer. Stir in the broth, beans and spinach. Stir in pasta, meatballs and remaining salt and pepper.

4. Cook until spinach is tender and meatballs are heated through. Garnish with remaining Parmesan cheese.

Wintertime Beef Soup

Kidney beans, ground beef, green pepper and chopped cabbage make a soup that's thick and satisfying.

— **CAROL TUPPER** JOPLIN, MISSOURI

PREP: 10 MIN. **COOK:** 55 MIN. **MAKES:** 8 SERVINGS (3¼ QUARTS)

- 1 pound lean ground beef (90% lean)
- 4 celery ribs, coarsely chopped
- 1 medium onion, coarsely chopped
- 1 medium green pepper, coarsely chopped
- 1 garlic clove, minced
- 2 cups water
- 2 cups reduced-sodium tomato juice
- 1 can (14½ ounces) diced tomatoes, undrained
- 1 can (8 ounces) tomato sauce
- 2 teaspoons reduced-sodium beef bouillon granules
- 2 teaspoons chili powder
- ½ teaspoon salt
- 2 cans (16 ounces each) kidney beans, rinsed and drained
- 2 cups chopped cabbage

1. In a Dutch oven, cook the beef, celery, onion, green pepper and garlic over medium heat until meat is no longer pink; drain. Stir in the water, tomato juice, tomatoes, tomato sauce, bouillon, chili powder and salt. Bring to a boil. Reduce heat; cover and simmer for 30 minutes.

2. Stir in kidney beans and cabbage; return to a boil. Reduce heat; cover and cook 12-15 minutes longer or until cabbage is tender.

Family Vegetable Beef Soup

My kids aren't excited about vegetables, but in this soup, they love them. It's an easy recipe to make.

— **LINDA KORTE** NEW LISKEARD, ONTARIO

PREP: 20 MIN. **COOK:** 1¼ HOURS
MAKES: 14 SERVINGS (3½ QUARTS)

- 2 pounds ground beef
- 1 medium onion, chopped
- 1 can (46 ounces) tomato juice

- 1 can (28 ounces) diced tomatoes, undrained
- 1 jar (4½ ounces) sliced mushrooms, drained
- 2 cups frozen cut green beans
- 2 cups each finely chopped celery, cabbage and carrots
- 1 teaspoon dried oregano
- 1 teaspoon dried basil
- ½ teaspoon garlic powder
- 1 teaspoon salt
- ½ teaspoon pepper

In a Dutch oven, cook beef and onion over medium heat until meat is no longer pink; drain. Stir in the remaining ingredients. Bring to a boil. Reduce heat; cover and simmer for 1 hour.

Hearty Wild Rice Soup

I tasted this thick and comforting soup at a food fair I helped judge. It didn't earn a ribbon, but I thought it was a real winner. The original recipe called for uncooked wild rice, but instead I use a quick-cooking rice blend.

— **KATHY HERINK** GLADBROOK, IOWA

PREP/TOTAL TIME: 20 MIN.
MAKES: 8 SERVINGS (ABOUT 2 QUARTS)

- 1 pound ground beef
- 2 cups chopped celery
- 2 cups chopped onions
- 3 cups water
- 1 can (14½ ounces) chicken broth
- 1 can (10¾ ounces) condensed cream of mushroom soup, undiluted
- 1 package (6¾ ounces) quick-cooking long grain and wild rice mix
- 5 bacon strips, cooked and crumbled

1. In a large saucepan, cook the beef, celery and onions over medium heat until meat is no longer pink and vegetables are tender; drain.

2. Add the water, broth, soup, rice and contents of the seasoning packet. Bring to a boil. Reduce heat; cover and simmer for 5 minutes or until heated through. Garnish with bacon.

Hamburger Garden Soup

PREP: 15 MIN. **COOK:** 45 MIN. **MAKES:** 5 SERVINGS

- 1 **pound ground beef**
- 1 **cup chopped onion**
- 1 **garlic clove, minced**
- 1 **can (28 ounces) diced tomatoes, undrained**
- 2 **cups fresh or frozen corn**
- 2 **cups water**
- 3 **tablespoons minced fresh parsley or 1 tablespoon dried parsley flakes**
- 2 **tablespoons minced fresh basil or 2 teaspoons dried basil**
- 2 **tablespoons minced fresh thyme or 2 teaspoons dried thyme**
- 1½ **teaspoons minced fresh rosemary or ½ teaspoon dried rosemary, crushed**
- 1 **teaspoon salt**
- ½ **teaspoon pepper**

In a large saucepan, cook the beef, onion and garlic over medium heat until meat is no longer pink; drain. Add the remaining ingredients; bring to a boil. Reduce heat; simmer, uncovered, for 30 minutes to allow flavors to blend.

66We have a large vegetable and herb garden and raise our own beef, so the only thing I need to buy for this soup is the garlic! Make the soup in summer, then freeze some for a hearty cold-weather meal.99

— **ALMA GRADY** FALLS CREEK, PENNSYLVANIA

Southwestern Goulash

I had some extra cilantro in the fridge and didn't want to throw it away. Instead, I came up with a Southwest-inspired soup using ingredients I had on hand. The whole family loved it.

— **VIKKI REBHOLZ** WEST CHESTER, OHIO

PREP/TOTAL TIME: 30 MIN. **MAKES:** 6 SERVINGS

- 1 **cup uncooked elbow macaroni**
- 1 **pound lean ground beef (90% lean)**
- 1 **medium onion, chopped**
- 1 **can (28 ounces) diced tomatoes, undrained**
- ⅔ **cup frozen corn**
- 1 **can (8 ounces) tomato sauce**
- 1 **can (4 ounces) chopped green chilies**
- ½ **teaspoon ground cumin**
- ½ **teaspoon pepper**
- ¼ **teaspoon salt**
- ¼ **cup minced fresh cilantro**

1. Cook the macaroni according to package directions. Meanwhile, in a Dutch oven over medium heat, cook beef and onion until meat is no longer pink; drain. Stir in the tomatoes, corn, tomato sauce, chilies, cumin, pepper and salt. Bring to a boil. Reduce heat; simmer, uncovered, for 3-4 minutes or until heated through.

2. Drain macaroni; add to meat mixture. Stir in cilantro and heat through.

Campfire Stew Packets

PREP: 15 MIN. **GRILL:** 25 MIN.
MAKES: 4 SERVINGS

- 1 egg, lightly beaten
- ¾ cup dry bread crumbs
- ¼ cup ketchup
- 1 tablespoon Worcestershire sauce
- 1 teaspoon seasoned salt
- 1 pound lean ground beef (90% lean)
- 2 cups frozen shredded hash brown potatoes, thawed
- 1 cup diced carrots
- 1 cup condensed cream of chicken soup, undiluted
- ¼ cup milk

1. Prepare grill for indirect heat. In a large bowl, combine the first five ingredients. Crumble beef over mixture and mix well. Shape into four patties. Place each patty on a greased double thickness of heavy-duty foil (about 12 in. square); sprinkle each with potatoes and carrots.

2. Combine soup and milk; spoon over meat and vegetables. Fold foil around mixture and seal tightly. Grill, covered, over indirect medium heat for 25-30 minutes or until meat is no longer pink and potatoes are tender. Open foil carefully to allow steam to escape.

Quick Pizza Soup

My kids first sampled this soup in the school cafeteria. They couldn't stop talking about it, so I knew I had to get the recipe. It's quick and easy to make.

— **PENNY LANXON** NEWELL, IOWA

PREP: 10 MIN. **COOK:** 35 MIN.
MAKES: 16 SERVINGS (4 QUARTS)

- 1 pound ground beef
- 2 cans (26 ounces each) condensed tomato soup, undiluted
- 6½ cups water
- 3½ cups spaghetti sauce
- 1 tablespoon Italian seasoning
- 2 cups (8 ounces) shredded cheddar cheese
  Additional shredded cheddar cheese, optional

1. In a Dutch oven, cook beef over medium heat until no longer pink; drain. Add the soup, water, spaghetti sauce and Italian seasoning; bring to a boil.

2. Reduce heat; simmer, uncovered, for 15 minutes. Stir in cheese until melted.

3. Garnish each serving with additional cheese if desired.

> These handy packets are perfect for grilling or whipping up over a campfire. I can get several outdoor chores done while they're cooking.
>
> — **MARGARET RILEY** TALLAHASSEE, FLORIDA

CAMPFIRE STEW PACKETS

❝ I made these sandwiches one evening for my family, and they were a huge hit with everyone, including the picky eaters. There's plenty of sauce and cheese to complement the baked meatballs. ❞

HEATHER BEGIN ATHENS, MAINE
about her recipe, Meatball Subs, on page 28

30

33

34

Sandwiches

Salsa Sloppy Joes

PREP/TOTAL TIME: 20 MIN.
MAKES: 8 SERVINGS

- 1 **pound ground beef**
- 1⅓ **cups salsa**
- 1 **can (10¾ ounces) condensed tomato soup, undiluted**
- 1 **tablespoon brown sugar**
- 8 **hamburger buns, split**

1. In a large skillet, cook beef over medium heat until no longer pink; drain. Stir in the salsa, soup and brown sugar. Cover and simmer for 10 minutes or until heated through.

2. Serve immediately on buns, or cool before placing in a freezer container. Cover and freeze for up to 3 months.

To use frozen Salsa Sloppy Joes: *Thaw in the refrigerator; place in a saucepan and heat through. Serve on buns.*

Mushroom Swiss Burgers

Easy skillet burgers heaping with rich mushrooms and Swiss cheese are perfect cold-weather fare. This recipe is sure to be requested often by your family.

— JAMES BOWLES IRONTON, OHIO

PREP/TOTAL TIME: 30 MIN.
MAKES: 6 SERVINGS

- 1½ **pounds ground beef**
- 1 **pound sliced fresh mushrooms**
- 1 **can (10¾ ounces) condensed cream of mushroom soup, undiluted**
- 1 **cup water**
- 6 **slices Swiss cheese**
- 6 **hamburger buns, split**

1. Shape the beef into six patties. In a large skillet, cook patties over medium-high heat for 5-7 minutes on each side or until a thermometer reads 160° and juices run clear.

2. Remove to paper towels; drain, reserving 2 tablespoons drippings. Saute mushrooms in drippings until tender.

3. Meanwhile, in a microwave-safe bowl, combine soup and water. Cover and microwave on high for 2½ to 3½ minutes or until heated through.

4. Return patties to the skillet. Stir in soup mixture. Bring to a boil. Reduce heat; simmer, uncovered, for 3 minutes.

5. Top each patty with a slice of cheese. Remove from the heat; cover and let stand until cheese is melted. Serve on buns topped with mushrooms.

I created these sandwiches when I realized I did not have a can of sloppy joe sauce. The sweet brown sugar in the recipe complements the tangy salsa.

— KRISTA COLLINS CONCORD, NORTH CAROLINA

SALSA SLOPPY JOES

Farmhouse Chili Dogs

We host lots of hay rides, picnics, hot dog roasts and ice cream socials on our farm, and these chili dogs never fail to please. There's always someone who fills a paper cup with the sauce and eats it straight.

— **CATHERINE BRALEY**
BARBOURSVILLE, WEST VIRGINIA

PREP: 15 MIN. **COOK:** 30 MIN.
MAKES: 8 SERVINGS

- 1 **pound ground beef**
- 1 **medium onion, chopped**
- 1 **can (10¾ ounces) condensed tomato soup, undiluted**
- ½ **cup water**
- 3 **tablespoons ketchup**
- 1 **tablespoon sugar**
- 1½ **teaspoons chili powder**
- 8 **hot dogs**
- 8 **hot dog buns, split**
  Shredded cheddar cheese, optional

1. In a large skillet, cook beef and onion over medium heat until meat is no longer pink; drain. Stir in the soup, water, ketchup, sugar and chili powder; bring to a boil. Reduce heat; simmer, uncovered, for 20 minutes or until thickened.
2. Cook hot dogs according to package directions. Place in buns; top with meat sauce. Sprinkle with cheese if desired.

All-American Barbecues

I came up with this delicious recipe on my own. It's my husband's favorite and is a big hit with family and friends who enjoyed it at our Fourth of July picnic.

— **SUE GRONHOLZ**
BEAVER DAM, WISCONSIN

PREP/TOTAL TIME: 25 MIN.
MAKES: 18 SERVINGS

- 4½ **pounds ground beef**
- 1½ **cups chopped onions**
- 2¼ **cups ketchup**
- 3 **tablespoons prepared mustard**
- 3 **tablespoons Worcestershire sauce**
- 2 **tablespoons vinegar**
- 2 **tablespoons sugar**
- 1 **tablespoon salt**
- 1 **tablespoon pepper**
- 18 **hamburger buns, split**

In a Dutch oven, cook beef and onions until meat is no longer pink and onion is tender; drain. Stir in the ketchup, mustard, Worcestershire sauce, vinegar, sugar, salt and pepper. Heat through. Serve on buns.

Bacon Cheeseburger Roll-Ups

PREP: 25 MIN. **BAKE:** 20 MIN. **MAKES:** 8 SERVINGS

- 1 **pound ground beef**
- 6 **bacon strips, diced**
- ½ **cup chopped onion**
- 1 **package (8 ounces) process cheese (Velveeta), cubed**
- 1 **tube (16.3 ounces) large refrigerated buttermilk biscuits**
- ½ **cup ketchup**
- ¼ **cup yellow mustard**

1. In a large skillet, cook the beef, bacon and onion over medium heat until meat is no longer pink; drain. Add cheese; cook and stir until melted. Remove from the heat.
2. Flatten each biscuit into a 5-in. circle; spoon ⅓ cup of the beef mixture onto each biscuit. Fold sides and ends over filling and roll up. Place seam side down on a greased baking sheet.
3. Bake at 400° for 18-20 minutes or until golden brown. In a small bowl, combine ketchup and mustard; serve with roll-ups.

“My husband and I both love these roll-ups. I often serve them with broccoli and cheese. They must be good, because this recipe won a first place prize at the Iowa State Fair!”

— **JESSICA CAIN** DES MOINES, IOWA

Flavorful Onion Burgers

The amount of flavor this burger packs with just a few simple ingredients will really surprise you. Cheddar cheese and Thousand Island dressing make them a real family treat.

— **DAVE BREMSON** PLANTATION, FLORIDA

PREP: 20 MIN. **GRILL:** 25 MIN. **MAKES:** 6 SERVINGS

- 1 **large onion**
- 1 **to 2 tablespoons olive oil**
  Salt and pepper to taste, optional
- ½ **cup chopped green pepper**
- ½ **cup shredded cheddar cheese**
- 2 **tablespoons minced fresh parsley**
- 1 **tablespoon Worcestershire sauce**
- 1½ **pounds ground beef**
- 6 **whole wheat hamburger buns, split**
- 6 **tablespoons prepared Thousand Island salad dressing**
- 6 **lettuce leaves**
- 6 **slices tomato**

1. Slice onion into ½-in.-thick rings; thread onto metal or soaked wooden skewers. Brush with oil. Season with salt and pepper if desired. Grill, covered, over medium-hot heat for 8-10 minutes on each side.

2. Meanwhile, in a large bowl, combine the green pepper, cheese, parsley and Worcestershire sauce. Crumble beef over mixture and mix well. Shape into six patties.

3. Move onion to indirect heat. Place burgers over direct heat. Cover and grill for 10-14 minutes or until meat is no longer pink and onion is tender, turning burgers once.

4. Spread bun bottoms with dressing; top each with lettuce, tomato, onion and a burger. Replace bun tops.

Meatball Subs

I made these sandwiches one evening for my family, and they were a huge hit with everyone, including the picky eaters. There's plenty of sauce and cheese to complement the baked meatballs.

— **HEATHER BEGIN** ATHENS, MAINE

PREP: 40 MIN. **BAKE:** 5 MIN. **MAKES:** 6-7 SERVINGS

- 1 **egg, lightly beaten**
- ⅓ **cup steak sauce**
- 1 **cup crushed saltines**
- 1 **teaspoon onion powder**
- ¼ **teaspoon seasoned salt**
- ⅛ **teaspoon pepper**
- 1½ **pounds ground beef**
- 6 **to 7 tablespoons mayonnaise**
- 6 **to 7 submarine buns, split**
- 9 **to 11 slices process American cheese, cut into strips**
- 1 **jar (14 ounces) pizza sauce**
- 2 **cups (8 ounces) shredded part-skim mozzarella cheese**

1. In a large bowl, combine the egg, steak sauce, saltines, onion powder, seasoned salt and pepper. Crumble beef over mixture and mix well. Shape into 1½-in. balls.

2. Place meatballs on a greased rack in a shallow baking pan. Bake at 375° for 20-25 minutes or until no longer pink. Drain on paper towels.

3. Spread mayonnaise over bun bottoms; top each with American cheese, 1 tablespoon pizza sauce, meatballs and remaining pizza sauce. Sprinkle with mozzarella cheese. Place on a baking sheet. Bake for 5-10 minutes or until cheese is melted.

top tip Preparing meatballs in bulk cuts back on prep time. I often make as many as five dinners' worth of meatballs in one evening. Then I freeze the cooked meatballs for quick dinners.

—**CHRISTI G.** TULSA, OKLAHOMA

French Tarragon Burgers

These hamburgers show off an innovative twist on a traditional burger that will have you licking your lips. The delightful sauce and crunchy French bread are delicious.

— **MICHAEL COHEN** LOS ANGELES, CALIFORNIA

PREP/TOTAL TIME: 30 MIN. **MAKES:** 6 SERVINGS

- 1 cup mayonnaise
- 2 tablespoons Dijon mustard
- 3 teaspoons chopped shallot, divided
- 2 teaspoons minced fresh tarragon or ¾ teaspoon dried tarragon
- 2 garlic cloves, minced
- 2 loaves (1 pound each) unsliced French bread
- 1 teaspoon salt
- ½ teaspoon pepper
- 2 pounds ground beef
- 4 cups spring mix salad greens

1. In a small bowl, combine the mayonnaise, mustard, 1 teaspoon shallot, tarragon and garlic; cover and refrigerate.

2. Meanwhile, cut the bread into six 4-in. lengths (save remaining bread for another use). Cut bread pieces in half horizontally; set aside.

3. Crumble beef into a large bowl; sprinkle with salt, pepper and remaining shallot. Shape into six patties.

4. Grill the burgers, covered, over medium heat for 6-8 minutes on each side or until a thermometer reads 160° and juices run clear.

5. Grill bread, cut side down, for 1-2 minutes or until toasted. Spread with mayonnaise mixture. Layer bread bottoms with greens and burgers. Replace tops.

Cheeseburger Meat Loaf Hoagies

PREP: 20 MIN. **BAKE:** 30 MIN. **MAKES:** 8 SANDWICHES

- 1 egg, lightly beaten
- 1 can (8 ounces) tomato sauce
- 1 cup quick-cooking oats
- ¼ cup chopped onion
- ½ teaspoon salt
- ½ teaspoon pepper
- 1½ pounds ground beef
- ⅓ cup mayonnaise
- 2 tablespoons ketchup
- 2 medium tomatoes, sliced
- 8 slices cheddar cheese
- 8 bacon strips, cooked and halved
- 8 hoagie buns, split and toasted

1. In a large bowl, combine the egg, tomato sauce, oats, onion, salt and pepper. Crumble beef over mixture and mix well. Press evenly into an ungreased 13-in. x 9-in. baking dish.

2. Bake, uncovered, at 350° for 30-35 minutes or until no pink remains and a thermometer reads 160°; drain.

3. Combine mayonnaise and ketchup; spread over meat loaf. Cut into eight rectangles; top each with tomato, cheese and bacon. Place on a baking sheet; broil 3-4 in. from the heat for 2-3 minutes or until cheese is melted. Serve on buns.

❝ I worked as a school cook for 15 years, and love to try new recipes. I've yet to find a better meat loaf than this. ❞

— **CONNIE BOUCHER** DIXON, MISSOURI

Pizza Joes

PREP/TOTAL TIME: 30 MIN.
MAKES: 6 SERVINGS

- 1   pound lean ground beef (90% lean)
- 1   can (15 ounces) pizza sauce
- 1   teaspoon dried oregano
- ½   medium onion
- ½   medium green pepper
- 1   ounce sliced pepperoni
- 6   hamburger buns, split
- ½   cup shredded mozzarella cheese
- ½   cup sliced fresh mushrooms

1. In a large skillet over medium heat, cook beef until no longer pink; drain. Stir in pizza sauce and oregano.

2. In a food processor, combine the onion, pepper and pepperoni; cover and process until chopped. Add to beef mixture. Simmer 20-25 minutes or until vegetables are tender. Spoon mixture onto buns. Top with cheese and mushrooms.

Firecracker Burgers

These tasty stuffed burgers are perfect fare for gatherings throughout the year. They're great with a cool, creamy macaroni salad and an icy cold drink.

— KELLY WILLIAMS
FORKED RIVER, NEW JERSEY

PREP: 20 MIN.   **GRILL:** 15 MIN.
MAKES: 4 SERVINGS

- 1   pound lean ground beef (90% lean)
- ¼   cup chunky salsa
- 4   frozen breaded cheddar cheese jalapeno peppers, thawed
- 4   hamburger buns, split and toasted
- ¼   cup guacamole
- 4   lettuce leaves
- ¼   cup salsa con queso dip
- ¼   cup sliced plum tomatoes
- 2   tablespoons sliced ripe olives
- 4   thin slices sweet onion

1. In a large bowl, combine the beef and salsa. Shape into four patties. Place a jalapeno in the center of each; wrap beef around jalapeno, forming a ball. Reshape into patties, about 3½ to 4 in. in diameter and 1 in. thick.

2. Grill the burgers, covered, over medium-hot heat for 7-8 minutes on each side or until a thermometer reads 160° and juices run clear.

3. Spread bun tops with guacamole. On each bun bottom, layer lettuce, a burger, salsa con queso dip, tomatoes, olives and onion; replace tops.

These Italian-style sloppy joes are just fantastic. They can be prepared and held until everyone's settled and ready to eat.

— JOANNE SCHLABACH SHREVE, OHIO

PIZZA JOES

Cheese-Topped Sloppy Joes

I got the recipe for these quick-to-fix sandwiches from my Aunt Nellie. She used to serve them to the harvest crew on her farm. Microwaved leftovers taste delicious the next day.

— **MARY DEMPSEY** OVERLAND PARK, KANSAS

PREP/TOTAL TIME: 25 MIN.
MAKES: 6 SERVINGS

- 1 **pound ground beef**
- 2 **celery ribs, chopped**
- 1 **tablespoon chopped onion**
- 1 **tablespoon all-purpose flour**
- 1 **tablespoon brown sugar**
- ½ **teaspoon ground mustard**
- ¾ **cup ketchup**
- 6 **hamburger buns, split**
- 6 **slices Swiss cheese**

1. In a large skillet, cook the beef, celery and onion over medium heat until meat is no longer pink; drain. Stir in the flour, brown sugar, mustard and ketchup.
2. Bring to a boil. Reduce heat; simmer, uncovered, for 10 minutes, stirring occasionally. Serve on buns with cheese.

Horseradish Burgers

My husband and I love to grill burgers year-round. This variation with a creamy horseradish filling is a hit with our family and friends.

— **CHRIS ANDERSON** MORTON, ILLINOIS

PREP/TOTAL TIME: 30 MIN.
MAKES: 8 SERVINGS

- 2 **pounds ground beef**
- 2 **tablespoons steak sauce**
- ¾ **teaspoon seasoned salt**
- 1 **package (3 ounces) cream cheese, softened**
- 1 **to 2 tablespoons prepared horseradish**
- 1 **teaspoon prepared mustard**
- 8 **hamburger buns, split**

1. In a large bowl, combine beef, steak sauce and seasoned salt; mix well. Shape into 16 thin patties. In a small bowl, combine cream cheese, horseradish and mustard. Spoon about 1 tablespoonful into the center of half of the patties; top with the remaining patties. Press edges to seal.
2. Grill, covered, over medium-hot heat for 5-7 minutes on each side or until a thermometer reads 160° and juices run clear. Serve on buns.

Hot Italian Wraps

PREP/TOTAL TIME: 30 MIN. **MAKES:** 6 SERVINGS

- 1 **pound ground beef**
- 1 **medium green pepper, chopped**
- ⅓ **cup chopped onion**
- 1 **can (8 ounces) pizza sauce**
- 30 **slices pepperoni**
- ½ **teaspoon dried oregano**
- 6 **flour tortillas (10 inches), warmed**
- 6 **pieces (1 ounce each) string cheese**

1. In a large skillet, cook the beef, green pepper and onion over medium heat until meat is no longer pink; drain. Stir in the pizza sauce, pepperoni and oregano.
2. Spoon about ½ cup beef mixture off-center on a tortilla; top with a piece of string cheese. Fold one side of tortilla over filling and roll up from the opposite side. Repeat.
3. Place seam side down on an ungreased baking sheet. Bake at 350° for 10 minutes or until cheese is melted.

"The kids will love these pepperoni and beef wraps. They're easy to assemble because each tortilla is simply tucked around a portion of hearty meat filling and a piece of string cheese."

— **TASTE OF HOME TEST KITCHEN**

Smothered Onion Patty Melts

I created a patty melt loaded with onions and Swiss cheese on flavorful toasted rye bread. I especially like to make these sandwiches with burgers hot off the grill, but you can broil them, too.

— **MARGIE JARVIS** DECATUR, TENNESSEE

PREP: 30 MIN. **GRILL:** 10 MIN. **MAKES:** 4 SERVINGS

- 2 medium onions, sliced
- 1 teaspoon canola oil
- ⅛ teaspoon plus ½ teaspoon salt, divided
- ¼ teaspoon pepper, divided
- 2 teaspoons Dijon mustard
- 1 garlic clove, minced
- ¼ teaspoon dried thyme
- ¼ teaspoon dried oregano
- 1 pound ground beef or turkey
- 8 slices rye bread, toasted
- 4 slices Swiss cheese

1. In a large nonstick skillet, saute onions in oil for 3 minutes. Sprinkle with ⅛ teaspoon salt and ⅛ teaspoon pepper. Reduce heat; cover and cook for 25-30 minutes or until onions are tender, stirring occasionally.

2. Meanwhile, in a large bowl, combine the mustard, garlic, thyme, oregano and remaining salt and pepper. Crumble beef over mixture and mix well. Shape into four patties.

3. Grill patties, covered, over medium heat or broil 4 in from the heat for 5-7 minutes on each side or until a thermometer reads 160° and juices run clear. Place each patty on a slice of toast; top with cheese, onions and remaining toast.

Reuben Burgers

If you're one of those folks who craves Reuben sandwiches, this yummy burger is made for you! It's a great supper with French fries and a green salad.

— **BERNICE MUILENBURG** MOLALLA, OREGON

PREP: 25 MIN. **COOK:** 10 MIN. **MAKES:** 4 SERVINGS

- 1 cup soft bread crumbs
- ⅔ cup Thousand Island salad dressing, divided
- 1 teaspoon salt

- ⅛ teaspoon pepper
- 1½ pounds ground beef
- 8 slices rye bread
- 1 can (14 ounces) sauerkraut, rinsed and drained
- 4 slices Swiss cheese
  Butter

1. In a large bowl, combine bread crumbs, ⅓ cup dressing, salt and pepper. Crumble beef over mixture and mix well. Shape into four oval patties, about ½ in. thick.

2. Broil 4 in. from the heat or pan-fry for 4-6 minutes on each side or until a thermometer reads 160° and juices run clear.

3. Place each on a slice of bread. Top with sauerkraut, cheese and remaining dressing and bread.

4. In a large skillet, melt 2-3 tablespoons butter. Toast sandwiches until lightly browned on both sides, adding butter if necessary.

Stuffed Bread Boat

While I was up with one of our babies more than 20 years ago, I heard this "secret" family recipe shared on an all-night talk show. None of our children or our growing troop of grandchildren ever passes up this special stuffed bread.

— **ELAINE BENT** MIDDLEBORO, MASSACHUSETTS

PREP: 25 MIN. **BAKE:** 20 MIN. **MAKES:** 6-8 SERVINGS

- 1 loaf (1 pound) unsliced Italian bread
- 1 pound ground beef
- 1 large onion, chopped
- 1 medium green pepper, chopped
- 1 cup chopped fresh spinach
- 1 medium tomato, chopped
- ½ teaspoon dried oregano
  Salt and pepper to taste

1. Cut a thin slice off the top of bread; set top aside. Hollow out the loaf, leaving a ¼-in. shell. Dice removed bread and set aside.

2. In a nonstick skillet, cook beef over medium heat until no longer pink; drain. Add the onion, green pepper, spinach and tomato; cook 3-4 minutes longer or until vegetables are crisp-tender. Stir in the oregano, salt, pepper, and diced bread.

3. Spoon into bread shell; replace top. Wrap tightly in heavy-duty foil. Bake at 400° for 20 minutes or until heated through. Cut into slices.

My mom always put her hamburger on top of a salad. I thought it was quite unusual as a child, but I adjusted the concept to make it a light and tasty meal for the whole family.

— **DEVON DELANEY** WESTPORT, CONNECTICUT

Beefstro Bruschetta Burgers

PREP/TOTAL TIME: 30 MIN.
MAKES: 4 SERVINGS

- 3 **tablespoons Dijon mustard**
- 3 **tablespoons reduced-sugar apricot preserves**
- 1 **tablespoon prepared horseradish**
- 2 **thin slices prosciutto or deli ham, chopped**
- 1 **pound lean ground beef (90% lean)**
- ¾ **teaspoon salt-free lemon-pepper seasoning**
- 8 **slices French bread (½ inch thick)**
- 1 **cup fresh arugula or baby spinach**
- 2 **ounces Brie cheese, cut into eight thin slices**
- ¼ **cup julienned roasted sweet red peppers**

1. In a small bowl, combine the mustard, preserves and horseradish. In a small skillet coated with cooking spray, cook and stir prosciutto over medium heat until lightly browned. Set aside.

2. In a large bowl, combine ground beef and lemon-pepper. Shape mixture into eight patties.

3. Moisten a paper towel with cooking oil; using long-handled tongs, lightly coat the grill rack.

4. Grill burgers, covered, over medium heat or broil 4 in. from heat for 3-4 minutes on each side or until a thermometer reads 160° and juices run clear. Remove and keep warm.

5. Grill or broil bread for 1-2 minutes on each side or until toasted.

6. Spread each slice of toast with 1¼ teaspoons reserved mustard sauce. Layer each with arugula, a burger, a cheese slice and 1¼ teaspoons additional sauce. Garnish with peppers and prosciutto. Serve immediately.

top tip When mixing and shaping burgers, meat loaves and meatballs, handle the ground beef mixture as little as possible. This ensures the final product will be light in texture, not dense or crumbly.

BEEFSTRO BRUSHETTA BURGERS

Stuffed Burgers on Portobellos

PREP/TOTAL TIME: 30 MIN.
MAKES: 4 SERVINGS

- 1 teaspoon Worcestershire sauce
- ½ teaspoon salt
- ½ teaspoon pepper
- 1⅓ pounds ground beef
- ½ cup shredded cheddar cheese
- 5 bacon strips, cooked and crumbled
- 4 large portobello mushrooms (about 4 inches), stems removed
- 1 tablespoon olive oil
- 4 tomato slices
- 4 lettuce leaves

1. In a large bowl, combine the Worcestershire sauce, salt and pepper. Crumble beef over mixture; mix well. Shape into eight thin patties. Combine cheese and bacon. Spoon into center of four patties. Top with remaining patties; press edges firmly to seal.

2. Grill burgers, covered, over medium heat for 6 minutes on each side or until a thermometer reads 160° and the juices run clear.

3. Meanwhile, brush mushroom caps with oil. Grill, covered, over medium heat for 3-4 minutes on each side or until tender. Top each mushroom cap with tomato, lettuce and a burger.

Pizza Burgers

Italian-seasoned beef patties are stuffed with cheese and treated to pizza toppings.

— **TASTE OF HOME TEST KITCHEN**

PREP/TOTAL TIME: 30 MIN.
MAKES: 2 SERVINGS

- ½ teaspoon minced garlic
- ½ teaspoon beef bouillon granules
- ½ teaspoon Italian seasoning
- ¼ teaspoon salt
- ½ pound ground beef
- 2 slices part-skim mozzarella cheese
- 2 hamburger buns, split
- 3 tablespoons pizza sauce, warmed
- 4 green pepper rings

1. Combine garlic, bouillon, Italian seasoning and salt; crumble beef over mixture and mix well. Shape into four thin patties. Place a cheese slice on two patties; top with another patty. Press edges to seal.

2. Grill, covered, over medium-hot heat for 6-8 minutes on each side or until a thermometer reads 160°. Serve on buns with pizza sauce and pepper rings.

Here's a low-carb treat that allows my husband and me to have burgers without compromising any succulent flavor. It's actually a combo of several recipes pulled together into one—and no one misses the bun.

— **DEBBIE DRIGGERS** GREENVILLE, TEXAS

STUFFED BURGERS ON PORTABELLOS

44

40

36

Stovetop
Suppers

Zesty Tacos

PREP/TOTAL TIME: 30 MIN.
MAKES: 8 SERVINGS

- 1 **pound ground beef**
- 1 **cup water**
- 1 **envelope taco seasoning**
- 8 **taco shells**
- 1 **can (15½ ounces) black-eyed peas, rinsed and drained**
- 1 **cup chopped tomatoes**
- 1 **cup shredded lettuce**
- 1 **cup (4 ounces) shredded cheddar cheese**
- ½ **cup zesty Italian salad dressing**

1. In a large skillet, cook beef over medium heat until no longer pink; drain. Stir in water and taco seasoning. Bring to a boil. Reduce heat; simmer, uncovered, for 4-5 minutes or until thickened.

2. Meanwhile, prepare taco shells according to package directions. Stir peas into skillet; heat through.

3. Spoon ¼ cup beef mixture into each taco shell. Top with tomatoes, lettuce and cheese. Drizzle with salad dressing.

Summer Harvest Stir-Fry

I work full-time outside the home, so I'm always trying fast-to-fix dishes. This colorful skillet supper appeals to the whole family, and I like that it uses lots of abundant summer vegetables.

— **KAY TOON** WORTHINGTON, INDIANA

PREP/TOTAL TIME: 25 MIN.
MAKES: 8-10 SERVINGS

- 1 **pound ground beef**
- 1 **medium onion, chopped**
- 6 **small yellow summer squash, chopped**
- 6 **medium tomatoes, quartered**
- 1½ **cups whole kernel corn**
- 1 **tablespoon minced fresh oregano or**
  - 1 **teaspoon dried oregano**
- 1 **teaspoon salt**
- ½ **teaspoon coarsely ground pepper**

1. In a large skillet, cook beef and onion over medium heat until meat is no longer pink; drain.

2. Add the summer squash, tomatoes, corn, oregano, salt and pepper. Cook and stir for 5-10 minutes or until the vegetables are tender.

Jazz up everyday tacos in a snap! Black-eyed peas and a drizzle of Italian dressing are the surprise ingredients that perk up my recipe.

— **SUSIE BONHAM** FAIRVIEW, OKLAHOMA

ZESTY TACOS

Stovetop Chili Casserole

Sometimes I add corn to my skillet chili to make it even more hearty and to give it more color. Throw in whatever quick-cooking vegetables you like.

— **RHONDA HOGAN** EUGENE, OREGON

PREP/TOTAL TIME: 25 MIN.
MAKES: 6 SERVINGS

- 1 pound ground beef
- ½ cup chopped onion
- 1 can (16 ounces) kidney beans, rinsed and drained
- 1 can (15 ounces) tomato sauce
- 1 can (14½ ounces) stewed tomatoes, undrained
- ¼ teaspoon garlic powder
- ¼ teaspoon salt
- ¼ teaspoon pepper
- 2 cups cooked noodles

In a large skillet, cook beef and onion over medium heat until meat is no longer pink; drain. Stir in the beans, tomato sauce, tomatoes, garlic powder, salt and pepper. Simmer, uncovered, for 5 minutes. Stir in noodles; heat through.

Asian Beef and Noodles

This yummy, economical dish takes only five ingredients—all of which you're likely to have on hand. Serve with a dash of soy sauce and a side of pineapple slices. Or try with ground turkey instead of beef.

— **LAURA STENBERG** WYOMING, MINNESOTA

PREP/TOTAL TIME: 20 MIN.
MAKES: 4 SERVINGS

- 1 pound lean ground beef (90% lean)
- 2 packages (3 ounces each) Oriental ramen noodles, crumbled
- 2½ cups water
- 2 cups frozen broccoli stir-fry vegetable blend
- ¼ teaspoon ground ginger
- 2 tablespoons thinly sliced green onion

1. In a large skillet, cook beef over medium heat until no longer pink; drain. Add the contents of one ramen noodle flavoring packet; stir until dissolved. Remove beef and set aside.
2. In the same skillet, combine the water, vegetables, ginger, noodles and contents of remaining flavoring packet. Bring to a boil. Reduce heat; cover and simmer for 3-4 minutes or until noodles are tender, stirring occasionally. Return beef to the pan and heat through. Stir in onion.

Three-Pepper Beef Wraps

Here's a versatile recipe with less than 400 calories per serving. Quick, simple to fix and good for you, it's a meal all ages seem to love.

— **DOREEN MUENCH** CHANDLER, ARIZONA

PREP: 25 MIN. **COOK:** 20 MIN. **MAKES:** 6 SERVINGS

- 1 each large green, sweet red and yellow peppers, julienned
- 1 medium onion, halved and sliced
- 2 tablespoons olive oil, divided
- ¾ pound lean ground beef (90% lean)
- 1 can (16 ounces) kidney beans, rinsed and drained
- ¾ cup salsa
- ¼ teaspoon steak seasoning
- ¼ teaspoon pepper
- 6 flour tortillas (8 inches), warmed
- ½ cup shredded reduced-fat cheddar cheese

1. In a large nonstick skillet, saute peppers and onion in 1 tablespoon oil until crisp-tender. Remove and keep warm.
2. In the same skillet, cook beef over medium heat until no longer pink; drain. Place the kidney beans, salsa and remaining oil in a food processor; cover and process until chopped. Add to beef. Sprinkle with steak seasoning and pepper; cook and stir until heated through.
3. Spoon about ⅓ cup beef mixture down the center of each tortilla; top each with ½ cup pepper mixture. Sprinkle with cheese. Fold sides and ends over filling and roll up.

Editor's Note: *This recipe was tested with McCormick's Montreal Steak Seasoning. Look for it in the spice aisle.*

Asparagus Mushroom Stir-Fry

Asparagus and shiitake mushrooms lend fresh flavor to a zesty homemade stir-fry sauce. Try with regular mushrooms if your store doesn't have shiitakes.

— TASTE OF HOME TEST KITCHEN

PREP/TOTAL TIME: 25 MIN. **MAKES:** 4 SERVINGS

- 1 pound lean ground beef (90% lean)
- 2 cups cut fresh asparagus (1-inch pieces)
- 1 can (8 ounces) sliced water chestnuts, drained
- ⅓ pound sliced fresh shiitake mushrooms
- 1 teaspoon minced garlic
- 2 teaspoons sesame oil
- 2 tablespoons cornstarch
- 1½ cups beef broth
- ⅓ cup hoisin sauce
- 2 tablespoons reduced-sodium soy sauce
- 1 teaspoon minced fresh gingerroot
- 1 large tomato, chopped
  Hot cooked rice, optional

1. In a large skillet or wok, cook beef over medium heat until no longer pink; drain and set aside. In the same pan, stir-fry the asparagus, water chestnuts, mushrooms and garlic in oil for 5 minutes or until crisp-tender.

2. In a small bowl, combine cornstarch and broth until smooth. Stir in the hoisin sauce, soy sauce and ginger. Pour over vegetables. Return beef to the pan. Bring to a boil; cook and stir for 2 minutes or until thickened. Remove from the heat; stir in tomato. Serve with rice if desired.

Saucy Beef Patties

These tender patties are sure to be a favorite with your family. They're so easy. I especially like to serve them with potato salad and baked beans. Or in the colder months, enjoy these saucy patties with mashed potatoes.

— BERNICE MORRIS MARSHFIELD, MISSOURI

PREP/TOTAL TIME: 30 MIN. **MAKES:** 4 SERVINGS

- 1 egg, lightly beaten
- ½ cup soft bread crumbs
- ½ teaspoon salt
- ¼ teaspoon pepper
- 1 pound ground beef
- 1 can (8 ounces) tomato sauce
- 2 tablespoons chopped green onion
- 2 tablespoons brown sugar
- 1 teaspoon Worcestershire sauce
- 1 teaspoon prepared yellow mustard

1. In a large bowl, combine the egg, bread crumbs, salt and pepper. Crumble beef over mixture and mix well. Shape into four patties. In a large skillet, brown patties on both sides. Remove and set aside; drain drippings.

2. In the same skillet, combine the remaining ingredients. Return patties to the skillet. Bring to a boil. Reduce heat; simmer, uncovered, for 10 minutes or until a thermometer reads 160°.

top tip
For successful stir-frying, chop and measure all ingredients before you start cooking. Begin by stir-frying meat. When it's cooked through, set meat aside. Stir-fry the vegetables, adding oil if necessary. Return meat to the pan and stir in the sauce ingredients. Complete the stir-fry by adding fast-cooking vegetables like tomatoes.

Bacon Cheeseburger Pasta

I try to make foods that are not only kid friendly, but are also easy to reheat since my husband works long hours and often eats later than our children. If you like, use reduced-fat cheese and ground turkey for a lighter version.

— **MELISSA STEVENS** ELK RIVER, MINNESOTA

PREP/TOTAL TIME: 30 MIN.
MAKES: 4-6 SERVINGS

- 8 ounces uncooked penne pasta
- 1 pound ground beef
- 6 bacon strips, diced
- 1 can (10¾ ounces) condensed tomato soup, undiluted
- 1 cup (4 ounces) shredded cheddar cheese
  Barbecue sauce and prepared mustard, optional

1. Cook pasta according to package directions. Meanwhile, in a large skillet, cook beef over medium heat until no longer pink; drain and set aside.

2. In the same skillet, cook bacon until crisp; remove with a slotted spoon to paper towels to drain. Discard drippings. Drain pasta; add to the skillet. Stir in the soup, beef and bacon; heat through.

3. Remove from the heat and sprinkle with cheese. Cover and let stand for 2-3 minutes or until the cheese is melted. Serve with barbecue sauce and mustard if desired.

Indian Fry Bread Tacos

PREP: 20 MIN. + STANDING **COOK:** 15 MIN. **MAKES:** 2 SERVINGS

- ¾ cup all-purpose flour
- ½ teaspoon baking powder
- ¼ teaspoon salt
- ⅓ cup hot water
- ½ pound lean ground beef (90% lean)
- 2 tablespoons taco seasoning
- ⅓ cup water
  Oil for frying
- 2 tablespoons chopped lettuce
- 2 tablespoons chopped tomato
- 2 tablespoons salsa
- 2 tablespoons sour cream

1. In a small bowl, combine the flour, baking powder and salt; stir in hot water to form a soft dough. Cover and let stand for 1 hour.

2. In a small skillet, cook beef over medium heat until no longer pink; drain. Stir in taco seasoning and water; simmer, uncovered, for 10 minutes. Keep warm.

3. Divide dough in half. On a lightly floured surface, roll each portion into a 4-in. circle.

4. In an electric skillet, heat 1 in. of oil to 350°. Fry bread circles in hot oil for 3-4 minutes on each side or until golden; drain on paper towels. Top each with meat mixture, lettuce and tomato. Serve with salsa and sour cream.

“Our son-in-law is half Comanche and half Kiowa, and this recipe is similar to one he uses. I downsized it for two.”

— **LADONNA REED** PONCA CITY, OKLAHOMA

Greek-Style Ravioli

Here's a flavorful Greek twist on an Italian classic. It's an easy weekday meal that's become one of our favorites. My husband and I enjoy it with garlic cheese toast.

— **HETTI WILLIAMS** RAPID CITY, SOUTH DAKOTA

PREP/TOTAL TIME: 25 MIN. **MAKES:** 2 SERVINGS

- 12 frozen cheese ravioli
- ⅓ pound lean ground beef (90% lean)
- 1 cup canned diced tomatoes with basil, oregano and garlic
- 1 cup fresh baby spinach
- ¼ cup sliced ripe olives, drained
- ¼ cup crumbled feta cheese

1. Cook ravioli according to package directions. Meanwhile, in a small skillet, cook beef over medium heat until no longer pink; drain. Stir in tomatoes. Bring to a boil. Reduce heat; simmer, uncovered, for 10 minutes.

2. Drain ravioli. Add the ravioli, spinach and olives to the beef mixture; heat through. Sprinkle with feta cheese.

Chili Mac

This yummy skillet dinner combines my chili recipe with an easy pasta dish I make. I often serve it to company or take it to potlucks. Sometimes I add taco seasoning and black beans.

— **LEE DENEAU** LANSING, MICHIGAN

PREP/TOTAL TIME: 20 MIN. **MAKES:** 6 SERVINGS

- 1 cup uncooked elbow macaroni
- 1 pound ground beef
- 1 small green pepper, chopped
- 1 small onion, chopped

- 2 cans (15 ounces each) chili with beans
- 1 can (11 ounces) whole kernel corn, drained
- 1 cup (4 ounces) shredded cheddar cheese

1. Cook macaroni according to package directions.

2. Meanwhile, in a large skillet, cook the beef, green pepper and onion over medium heat until meat is no longer pink; drain. Stir in chili and corn. Drain macaroni; add to the skillet and heat through. Sprinkle with cheese.

Beefy Shells and Cheese

Here's a family-pleasing dinner that starts with boxed macaroni and cheese. I like to top it with shredded Monterey Jack or cheddar cheese for even more cheesy flavor.

— **LOUISE GRAYBIEL** TORONTO, ONTARIO

PREP/TOTAL TIME: 30 MIN. **MAKES:** 6 SERVINGS

- 1 pound ground beef
- 1 package (12 ounces) shells and cheese dinner mix
- 2 cups water
- 1¼ cups salsa
- 1 can (15 ounces) black beans, rinsed and drained
- 1 to 2 teaspoons chili powder
- ⅛ teaspoon salt

1. In a large skillet, cook beef over medium heat until no longer pink; drain. Set aside cheese sauce packet from dinner mix. Add shells and water to skillet. Bring to a boil; cover and simmer for 10-12 minutes or until pasta is tender.

2. Stir in the salsa, beans, chili powder, salt and contents of cheese sauce packet. Remove from the heat; cover and let stand for 5 minutes.

One evening, we had unexpected company. Since I had some of these meatballs left over in the freezer, I warmed them up as appetizers. Everyone raved! This classic recipe makes a big batch and is perfect for entertaining.

— **MARY LOU KOSKELLA** PRESCOTT, ARIZONA

Best Spaghetti and Meatballs

PREP: 30 MIN. **COOK:** 2 HOURS
MAKES: 12-16 SERVINGS

- 1½ cups chopped onions
- 2 tablespoons olive oil
- 3 garlic cloves, minced
- 3 cups water
- 1 can (29 ounces) tomato sauce
- 2 cans (12 ounces each) tomato paste
- ⅓ cup minced fresh parsley
- 1 tablespoon dried basil
- 1 tablespoon salt
- ½ teaspoon pepper

MEATBALLS

- 4 eggs, lightly beaten
- 2 cups soft bread cubes (¼-inch pieces)
- 1½ cups milk
- 1 cup grated Parmesan cheese
- 3 garlic cloves, minced
- 1 tablespoon salt
- ½ teaspoon pepper
- 3 pounds ground beef
- 2 tablespoons canola oil
  Hot cooked spaghetti

1. In a Dutch oven over medium heat, saute onions in oil. Add garlic; cook 1 minute longer. Add the water, tomato sauce and paste, parsley, basil, salt and pepper; bring to a boil. Reduce heat; cover and simmer for 50 minutes.

2. In a large bowl, combine the first seven meatball ingredients. Crumble beef over mixture and mix well. Shape mixture into 1½-in. balls.

3. In a large skillet over medium heat, brown meatballs in batches in oil until no longer pink; drain. Add to sauce. Bring to a boil. Reduce heat; cover and simmer for 1 hour or until flavors are blended, stirring occasionally. Serve with spaghetti.

top tip

To prepare meatballs without having to stand over the stove turning each one, I arrange them on a greased broiler pan and bake at 350° for about 25 minutes. There's no need to turn them—they'll brown on all sides.

—**MARIAN S.**
ELKHORN, WISCONSIN

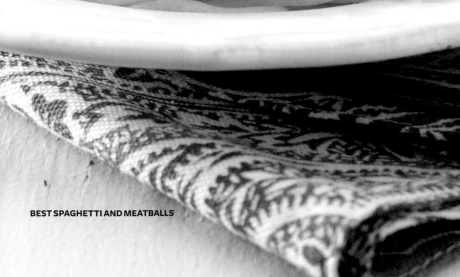

BEST SPAGHETTI AND MEATBALLS

Onion Salisbury Steak

Ground beef patties, tender onions and a rich gravy top toasted bread to make this Depression-era favorite. I've relied on the recipe for as long as I can remember.

— CLAUDINE MOFFATT MANCHESTER, MISSOURI

PREP/TOTAL TIME: 25 MIN. **MAKES:** 4 SERVINGS

- 1 **pound lean ground beef (90% lean)**
- ½ **teaspoon salt**
- ⅛ to ¼ **teaspoon pepper**
- 2 **medium onions, thinly sliced**
- 4 **slices bread, toasted**
- ¼ **cup all-purpose flour**
- 1½ **cups water**
- 1 **tablespoon beef bouillon granules**

1. In a large bowl, combine the beef, salt and pepper; shape into four oval patties. In a large skillet, brown patties on one side. Turn and add onions. Cook until a thermometer reads 160° and juices run clear. Place toast on serving plates. Top each slice with onions and a beef patty; keep warm.

2. Stir flour into skillet until blended. Gradually add water; stir in bouillon. Bring to a boil; cook and stir for 2 minutes or until thickened and bubbly. Serve with meat and onions.

Herbed Mushroom Spaghetti Sauce

Ground beef makes spaghetti sauce thick and hearty, and herbs give it wonderful flavor.

— ANNE HALFHILL SUNBURY, OHIO

PREP: 15 MIN. **COOK:** 1 HOUR **MAKES:** 6 SERVINGS

- 1 **pound lean ground beef (90% lean)**
- ½ **pound sliced fresh mushrooms**
- 1 **large onion, chopped**
- 1 **small green pepper, chopped**

- 2 **tablespoons olive oil**
- 4 **garlic cloves, minced**
- 2 **cans (8 ounces each) tomato sauce**
- 1 **can (10¾ ounces) condensed tomato soup, undiluted**
- 1 **teaspoon dried basil**
- ½ **teaspoon salt, optional**
- ½ **teaspoon dried rosemary, crushed**
- ½ **teaspoon dried oregano**
- ¼ **teaspoon pepper**
  Hot cooked spaghetti

In a large skillet, cook beef, mushrooms, onion and green pepper in oil over medium heat until meat is no longer pink. Add garlic; cook 1 minute longer. Drain. Stir in tomato sauce, soup and seasonings. Bring to a boil. Reduce heat; cover and simmer for 45-60 minutes, stirring occasionally. Serve with spaghetti.

Southwestern Wagon Wheels

My family loves this super-easy pasta dinner. It's great when I don't have the time to cook from scratch.

— RAMONA RASAS-SATINSKAS HOCKESSIN, DELAWARE

PREP/TOTAL TIME: 20 MIN. **MAKES:** 5 SERVINGS

- 4 **cups uncooked wagon wheel pasta**
- 1 **pound lean ground beef (90% lean)**
- 2 **cans (10¾ ounces each) condensed tomato soup, undiluted**
- 1 **cup medium salsa**
- 1 **jar (4½ ounces) sliced mushrooms, drained**
- 1 **teaspoon dried oregano**
- ½ **cup sour cream**
- ⅓ **cup shredded Monterey Jack cheese**

1. Cook pasta according to package directions. Meanwhile, in a large skillet, cook beef over medium heat until no longer pink; drain. Stir in the soup, salsa, mushrooms and oregano. Bring to a boil. Reduce heat; simmer, uncovered, for 5 minutes. Stir in sour cream; heat through.

2. Drain pasta; serve with sauce mixture. Sprinkle with cheese.

Garden Skillet

PREP/TOTAL TIME: 30 MIN. **MAKES:** 6-8 SERVINGS

- 2   **pounds ground beef**
- 3   **medium zucchini, julienned**
- 4   **medium carrots, julienned**
- 1   **can (14 ounces) bean sprouts, drained**
- 1   **medium onion, cut into thin wedges**
- ¾   **cup julienned green pepper**
- 1   **medium tomato, cut into wedges**
- 1   **garlic clove, minced**
- 1   **teaspoon salt**
- 1   **teaspoon ground cumin**

In a large skillet, cook beef over medium heat until no longer pink; drain. Add the zucchini, carrots, bean sprouts, onion and green pepper. Cook and stir for 3-4 minutes or until crisp-tender. Add the tomato, garlic, salt and cumin; heat through.

"As part of our final exam in a cooking class, we had to improve upon an existing recipe and serve it to the other students. This was my class-approved creation."

— GALELYNN PETERSON LONG BEACH, CALIFORNIA

Beef Ragu with Ravioli

Here's a no-stress pasta sauce that tastes like it was simmering all day! Serve it over your favorite refrigerated or frozen ravioli for an easy meal maker.

— TASTE OF HOME TEST KITCHEN

PREP: 15 MIN. **COOK:** 40 MIN. **MAKES:** 4 SERVINGS

- 1   **pound ground beef**
- ½   **cup chopped onion**
- 1   **pound plum tomatoes, diced**
- 1   **cup beef broth**
- ½   **cup red wine or additional beef broth**
- 1   **can (6 ounces) tomato paste**
- 2   **teaspoons minced fresh rosemary**
- 1   **teaspoon sugar**
- 1   **teaspoon minced garlic**
- ½   **teaspoon salt**
- 1   **package (20 ounces) refrigerated cheese ravioli**
     Grated Parmesan cheese, optional

1. In a large skillet, cook beef and onion over medium heat until meat is no longer pink; drain. Add the tomatoes, broth, wine, tomato paste, rosemary, sugar, garlic and salt. Bring to a boil. Reduce heat; simmer, uncovered, for 30 minutes.

2. Cook ravioli according to package directions; drain. Serve with meat sauce. Sprinkle with cheese if desired.

Chimichangas

PREP/TOTAL TIME: 30 MIN.
MAKES: 6 SERVINGS

- 1 **pound ground beef**
- 1 **envelope taco seasoning**
- 1 **can (16 ounces) refried beans**
- 6 **flour tortillas (12 inches), warmed**
- 1 **cup (4 ounces) shredded Colby-Monterey Jack cheese**
- 4 **teaspoons canola oil**
  Sour cream and salsa

1. In a large skillet, cook beef over medium heat until no longer pink; drain. Stir in taco seasoning. In a small saucepan, cook refried beans over medium-low heat for 2-3 minutes or until heated through.

2. Spoon about ⅓ cup of beans off-center on each tortilla; top with ¼ cup beef mixture. Sprinkle with cheese. Fold sides and ends of tortilla over filling and roll up.

3. In a large skillet over medium-high heat, brown chimichangas in oil on all sides. Serve with sour cream and salsa.

Taco Salad Waffles

Here is a fresh twist on the usual fare. It's perfect for a build-your-own-taco party for teenagers, but I have also served it as a brunch dish.

— **TRISHA KRUSE** EAGLE, IDAHO

PREP/TOTAL TIME: 25 MIN.
MAKES: 4 SERVINGS

- 1 **pound ground beef**
- 1 **cup salsa**
- 1 **can (4 ounces) chopped green chilies**
- 1 **envelope taco seasoning**
- 8 **frozen waffles**
  Shredded cheddar cheese, shredded lettuce, chopped tomatoes, cubed avocado, salsa and sour cream, optional

1. In a large skillet, cook beef over medium heat until no longer pink; drain.

2. Stir in the salsa, chilies and taco seasoning. Bring to a boil. Reduce heat; simmer for 5 minutes.

3. Meanwhile, toast waffles according to package directions. Serve with beef mixture and the toppings of your choice.

My cousin is of Mexican heritage, and I've watched her make these crunchy and delicious wraps for years. The first time I made them for my own family, they became an instant favorite.

— **DEBI LANE** CHATTANOOGA, TENNESSEE

CHIMICHANGAS

Summer Stuffed Peppers

Living in the Willamette Valley, we've always had an abundance of fresh garden vegetables, and this recipe allows me to use many of them.

— **PAT WHITAKER** ALSEA, OREGON

PREP: 20 MIN. **COOK:** 30 MIN.
MAKES: 8 SERVINGS

- 8 medium yellow, green or sweet red peppers
- 1½ pounds lean ground beef (90% lean)
- 1 medium onion, minced
- ½ cup finely chopped cabbage
- 1 medium carrot, shredded
- ½ cup shredded zucchini
- ½ garlic clove, minced
- 1 can (28 ounces) diced tomatoes, undrained
- ½ cup uncooked long-grain rice
- 1 tablespoon brown sugar
- ¼ teaspoon dried basil
  Pepper to taste

1. Cut the tops off peppers and set aside. Cook peppers in boiling water until crisp-tender, about 2-3 minutes. Remove and rinse with cold water; set aside. Remove stems from pepper tops and chop enough of the tops to measure ⅓ cup. (Save remaining peppers for another use.)

2. In a large skillet, brown ground beef over medium heat; drain if necessary. Add the onion, cabbage, carrot, zucchini and reserved chopped peppers; saute until tender. Add garlic; cook 1 minute longer. Stir in the tomatoes, rice, brown sugar, basil and pepper. Bring to a boil. Reduce heat; simmer about 20 minutes or until rice is tender.

3. Stuff hot meat mixture into peppers; warm in the microwave if necessary. Serve immediately.

Spaghetti with Italian Meatballs

My family enjoys this hearty spaghetti dinner. The versatile sauce can be served over almost any type of pasta.

— **SHARON CRIDER** JUNCTION CITY, KANSAS

PREP: 20 MIN. **COOK:** 1¼ HOURS **MAKES:** 10 SERVINGS

- ¾ cup chopped onion
- 1 tablespoon olive oil
- 1 garlic clove, minced
- 1 can (28 ounces) Italian crushed tomatoes, undrained
- 1 can (6 ounces) tomato paste
- 1 cup water
- 1½ teaspoons dried oregano
- ½ teaspoon salt
- ½ teaspoon pepper

MEATBALLS

- 4 slices white bread, torn
- ½ cup water
- 2 eggs, lightly beaten
- ½ cup grated Parmesan cheese
- 1 garlic clove, minced
- 1 teaspoon dried basil
- 1 teaspoon dried parsley flakes
- ½ teaspoon salt
- 1 pound lean ground beef (90% lean)
- 2 teaspoons olive oil
- 1 package (16 ounces) spaghetti

1. In a large saucepan, cook onion in oil until tender. Add garlic; cook 1 minute longer. Stir in the tomatoes, tomato paste, water, oregano, salt and pepper. Bring to a boil. Reduce heat; cover and simmer for 30 minutes.

2. Meanwhile, in a small bowl, soak bread in water for 5 minutes. Squeeze out excess liquid. In a large bowl, combine the eggs, cheese, garlic, basil, parsley, salt and bread. Crumble beef over mixture and mix well. Shape into 1-in. balls.

3. In a large nonstick skillet coated with cooking spray, brown meatballs in batches in oil over medium heat.

4. Add meatballs to sauce; return to a boil. Reduce heat; simmer, uncovered, for 30 minutes or until meatballs are no longer pink.

5. Cook the spaghetti according to package directions; drain. Serve spaghetti with meatballs and sauce.

Greek-Style Supper

Here's a quick recipe that's different from the Italian-style skillets that are so popular. As a part-time college student who also works, I rely on easy dishes like these. Just add salad and rolls and you have a great dinner for your family.

— **ALICE BOWER** ROANOKE, ILLINOIS

PREP/TOTAL TIME: 30 MIN. **MAKES:** 4 SERVINGS

- ½ pound ground beef
- ½ cup chopped onion
- 1 can (14½ ounces) beef broth
- 1 can (14½ ounces) diced tomatoes, undrained
- 1½ cups uncooked penne pasta
- 1½ cups frozen cut green beans, thawed
- 2 tablespoons tomato paste
- 2 teaspoons dried oregano
- ½ teaspoon garlic powder
- ¼ teaspoon ground cinnamon
- ¾ cup crumbled feta cheese

1. In a large skillet, cook beef and onion over medium heat until meat is no longer pink. Meanwhile, in a large saucepan, bring broth and tomatoes to a boil; add pasta. Reduce heat; simmer, uncovered, for 15-20 minutes or until pasta is tender, stirring occasionally.

2. Drain beef mixture; add to pasta. Stir in the beans, tomato paste, oregano, garlic powder and cinnamon; heat through. Sprinkle with feta cheese.

Anytime Lasagna

PREP/TOTAL TIME: 30 MIN. **MAKES:** 6-8 SERVINGS

- 1 pound ground beef
- 1 can (14½ ounces) diced tomatoes, undrained
- 2 eggs, lightly beaten
- 1½ cups ricotta cheese
- 4 cups marinara sauce
- 1 package (9 ounces) no-cook lasagna noodles
- 1 cup (4 ounces) shredded part-skim mozzarella cheese, optional

1. In a large skillet, cook beef over medium heat until no longer pink; drain. Transfer to a large bowl; stir in tomatoes. In a small bowl, combine eggs and ricotta cheese.

2. Return 1 cup meat mixture to the skillet; spread evenly. Layer with 1 cup ricotta mixture, 1½ cups marinara sauce and half of the noodles, breaking noodles to fit as necessary. Repeat layers. Top with remaining marinara sauce.

3. Bring to a boil. Reduce heat; cover and simmer 15-17 minutes or until noodles are tender and a thermometer reads 160°.

4. Remove from the heat. Sprinkle with mozzarella cheese if desired; let stand for 2 minutes or until cheese is melted.

❝Thanks to no-cook noodles, my skillet lasagna is a fresh, filling, flavorful and fast Italian entree. You can enjoy lasagna at any time!❞

— **MEGHAN CRIHFIELD** RIPLEY, WEST VIRGINIA

Golden-brown hash brown patties get topped with beefy sloppy joe mix and other tasty toppers for a fun twist on dinner that the kids will love.

— TASTE OF HOME TEST KITCHEN

SLOPPY JOE HASH BROWNS

Sloppy Joe Hash Browns

PREP: 10 MIN. **COOK:** 25 MIN.
MAKES: 4 SERVINGS

- 8 frozen hash brown patties
- 1 pound ground beef
- ¼ cup chopped onion
- 1 can (15½ ounces) sloppy joe sauce
- 1 tablespoon chili sauce
- ¼ teaspoon pepper
- 1 cup (4 ounces) shredded part-skim mozzarella cheese
- 2 cups shredded lettuce
- 1 medium tomato, chopped

1. Cook hash browns in batches according to package directions.
2. Meanwhile, in a large skillet, cook beef and onion over medium heat until meat is no longer pink; drain. Add the sloppy joe sauce, chili sauce and pepper; cook and stir until heated through.
3. Place two hash brown patties on each plate; top with meat sauce, cheese, lettuce and tomato.

Popeye Special

Spinach packs my own creation with a real Popeye punch, while the other vegetables combined with the ground beef and eggs make it a hearty, nutritious and economical meal. We enjoy this often.

— **MARCY CELLA** L'ANSE, MICHIGAN

PREP/TOTAL TIME: 20 MIN.
MAKES: 4-6 SERVINGS

- 1 pound ground beef
- ½ pound fresh mushrooms, sliced
- ½ pound fresh spinach, torn
- 6 green onions, sliced
- ¼ cup chopped celery
- ¼ cup chopped sweet red pepper
- 1 teaspoon garlic salt
- ½ teaspoon pepper
- 6 eggs, lightly beaten

1. In a large skillet, cook beef and mushrooms over medium heat until meat is no longer pink; drain.
2. Add the spinach, onions, celery, red pepper, garlic salt and pepper. Cook and stir for 1 minute.
3. Add eggs; cook and stir just until the eggs are set. Serve immediately.

Skillet Beef Tamales

This Southwestern skillet dinner is cheesy and delicious. Best of all, it's lighter than you'd imagine! It's sure to become a much-requested recipe in your house.

— **DEB WILLIAMS** PEORIA, ARIZONA

PREP/TOTAL TIME: 30 MIN. **MAKES:** 5 SERVINGS

- 1 **pound lean ground beef (90% lean)**
- ⅓ **cup chopped green pepper**
- ⅓ **cup chopped sweet red pepper**
- 2 **cups salsa**
- ¾ **cup frozen corn**
- 2 **tablespoons water**
- 6 **corn tortillas (6 inches), halved and cut into ½-inch strips**
- ¾ **cup shredded reduced-fat cheddar cheese**
- 5 **tablespoons fat-free sour cream**

1. In a large nonstick skillet coated with cooking spray, cook beef and peppers over medium heat until meat is no longer pink; drain. Stir in the salsa, corn and water; bring to a boil.

2. Stir in tortilla strips. Reduce heat; cover and simmer for 10-15 minutes or until tortillas are softened. Sprinkle with cheese; cover and cook 2-3 minutes longer or until cheese is melted. Serve with sour cream.

Mock Stroganoff

PREP/TOTAL TIME: 25 MIN. **MAKES:** 4 SERVINGS

- 3 **cups uncooked egg noodles**
- 1 **pound ground beef**
- ¼ **cup chopped onion**
- ¼ **cup sliced fresh mushrooms**
- 1½ **cups water**
- 2 **envelopes brown gravy mix**
- 2 **cups (16 ounces) sour cream**

1. Cook noodles according to package directions. Meanwhile, in a large skillet, cook the beef, onion and mushrooms over medium heat until meat is no longer pink; drain.

2. Stir in water and gravy mixes. Bring to a boil; cook and stir for 2 minutes or until thickened. Remove from the heat; stir in sour cream. Drain noodles. Serve with meat mixture.

❝I'm not a huge steak eater, but I've always loved the flavor of Stroganoff. Using hamburger in my version made it more palatable for me and an easy dish for our children to eat as toddlers.❞

— **TERRI WETZEL** ROSEBURG, OREGON

German Pizza

I like to serve this simple meal when family visits from Pennsylvania. Even if it's just my husband, our son and me around the table, German Pizza is a favorite.

— **AUDREY NOLT** VERSAILLES, MISSOURI

PREP: 20 MIN. **COOK:** 40 MIN. **MAKES:** 4-6 SERVINGS

- 1 pound ground beef
- ½ medium onion, chopped
- ½ green pepper, diced
- 1½ teaspoon salt, divided
- ½ teaspoon pepper
- 2 tablespoons butter
- 6 medium potatoes (about 2¼ pounds), peeled and finely shredded
- 3 eggs, lightly beaten
- ⅓ cup milk
- 2 cups (8 ounces) shredded cheddar or part-skim mozzarella cheese

1. In a large skillet over medium heat, cook and stir the beef, onion, green pepper, ½ teaspoon salt and pepper until meat is no longer pink; drain. Remove and keep warm.

2. Reduce heat to low; melt butter in pan. Spread potatoes over butter and sprinkle with remaining salt. Top with beef mixture. Combine eggs and milk; pour over all.

3. Cover and cook for 30 minutes or until set in the center. Sprinkle with the cheese; cover and cook until melted. Cut pizza into wedges.

Salisbury Steak with Gemelli

This streamlined classic has great flavor and appeal. Keep the recipe handy because this crowd-pleaser is ideal for busy weeknights.

— **TASTE OF HOME TEST KITCHEN**

PREP/TOTAL TIME: 30 MIN. **MAKES:** 4 SERVINGS

- 1 egg, beaten
- ½ cup soft bread crumbs
- 1 teaspoon Italian seasoning
- ½ teaspoon pepper
- ½ teaspoon minced garlic
- 1 pound ground beef
- 1 tablespoon olive oil
- 1 cup sliced fresh mushrooms
- 2 tablespoons all-purpose flour
- 1 cup chicken broth
- 1 tablespoon ketchup
- 1 teaspoon Worcestershire sauce
  Hot cooked gemelli or spiral pasta

1. In a large bowl, combine the egg, bread crumbs, Italian seasoning, pepper and garlic. Crumble beef over mixture and mix well. Shape into four patties.

2. In a large skillet, cook patties in oil over medium-high heat for 5-7 minutes on each side or until a thermometer reads 160° and juices run clear. Remove and keep warm.

3. Drain drippings, reserving 2 tablespoons in the pan. Saute mushrooms in drippings until tender. Stir in flour until blended. Gradually stir in the broth, ketchup and Worcestershire sauce. Bring to a boil; cook and stir for 2 minutes or until thickened.

4. Return patties to the skillet. Bring to a boil. Reduce heat; simmer, uncovered, for 3-4 minutes or until heated through. Serve with gemelli.

Hearty Penne Beef

PREP/TOTAL TIME: 30 MIN.
MAKES: 4 SERVINGS

- 1¾ cups uncooked penne pasta
- 1 pound ground beef
- 1 teaspoon minced garlic
- 1 can (15 ounces) tomato puree
- 1 can (14½ ounces) beef broth
- 1½ teaspoons Italian seasoning
- 1 teaspoon Worcestershire sauce
- ¼ teaspoon salt
- ¼ teaspoon pepper
- 2 cups chopped fresh spinach
- 2 cups (8 ounces) shredded part-skim mozzarella cheese

1. Cook pasta according to package directions. Meanwhile, in a Dutch oven, cook beef over medium heat until no longer pink. Add garlic; cook 1 minute longer. Drain. Stir in the tomato puree, broth, Italian seasoning, Worcestershire sauce, salt and pepper.
2. Bring to a boil. Reduce heat; simmer, uncovered, for 10-15 minutes or until slightly thickened. Add spinach; cook for 1-2 minutes or until spinach is wilted.
3. Drain pasta; stir into beef mixture. Sprinkle with cheese; cover and cook for 3-4 minutes or until cheese is melted.

Stovetop Beef 'n' Shells

I fix this supper when I'm pressed for time. It's as tasty as it is fast. Team it with salad, bread and fruit for a comforting meal.
— **DONNA ROBERTS** MANHATTAN, KANSAS

PREP/TOTAL TIME: 30 MIN.
MAKES: 4 SERVINGS

- 1½ cups uncooked medium pasta shells
- 1 pound lean ground beef (90% lean)
- 1 medium onion, chopped
- 1 garlic clove, minced
- 1 can (15 ounces) crushed tomatoes
- 1 can (8 ounces) tomato sauce
- 1 teaspoon sugar
- ½ teaspoon salt
- ½ teaspoon pepper

1. Cook pasta according to package directions. Meanwhile, in a large saucepan, cook beef and onion over medium heat until meat is no longer pink. Add garlic; cook 1 minute longer. Drain.
2. Stir in the tomatoes, tomato sauce, sugar, salt and pepper. Bring to a boil. Reduce heat; simmer, uncovered, for 10-15 minutes. Drain pasta; stir into beef mixture and heat through.

This is comfort food at its finest! The best of everything is found here—it's tasty, easy and a great way to sneak in some spinach for extra nutrition.
— **TASTE OF HOME TEST KITCHEN**

HEARTY PENNE BEEF

Taco Macaroni

My satisfying macaroni dish uses all the ingredients of stuffed peppers, but in an easy one-dish meal. For a saucier variation, use two cans of tomato soup or sauce. You might like it with canned kidney beans, too.

— MARISSA UNDERCOFLER
HOWARD, PENNSYLVANIA

PREP/TOTAL TIME: 30 MIN.
MAKES: 6 SERVINGS

- 1 package (16 ounces) elbow macaroni
- 1 pound ground beef
- ¾ cup chopped onion
- 1 can (14½ ounces) diced tomatoes, undrained
- 1 can (10¾ ounces) condensed tomato soup, undiluted
- 1 can (8 ounces) tomato sauce
- 1 envelope taco seasoning
  Shredded cheddar cheese

1. Cook macaroni according to package directions. Meanwhile, in a Dutch oven, cook beef and onion over medium heat until meat is no longer pink; drain.
2. Stir in the tomatoes, soup, tomato sauce and taco seasoning. Bring to a boil. Reduce heat; simmer, uncovered, for 8-10 minutes or until thickened.
3. Drain macaroni; stir into meat mixture and heat through. Sprinkle with cheese.

Beefy Tomato Rice Skillet

I put this together one day with what I had on hand. It's quick on busy nights or in the summer when we're camping.

— ELLYN GRAEBERT YUMA, ARIZONA

PREP/TOTAL TIME: 25 MIN.
MAKES: 6 SERVINGS

- 1 pound ground beef
- 1 cup chopped celery
- ⅔ cup chopped onion
- ½ cup chopped green pepper
- 1 can (11 ounces) whole kernel corn, drained
- 1 can (10¾ ounces) condensed tomato soup, undiluted
- 1 cup water
- 1 teaspoon Italian seasoning
- 1 cup uncooked instant rice

1. In a large skillet over medium heat, cook the beef, celery, onion and pepper until meat is no longer pink and vegetables are tender; drain.
2. Add the corn, soup, water and Italian seasoning; bring to a boil. Stir in rice; cover and remove from the heat. Let stand for 10 minutes or until rice is tender.

Burritos Made Easy

PREP/TOTAL TIME: 30 MIN. **MAKES:** 8 BURRITOS

- 1 pound ground beef
- ¼ cup chopped onion
- 1 can (15 ounces) chili with beans
- 1¼ cups chunky salsa
- ¼ cup canned chopped green chilies
- 8 flour tortillas (8 inches), warmed
- 8 slices process American cheese
  Taco sauce and shredded lettuce, optional

1. In a large skillet, cook beef and onion over medium heat until meat is no longer pink; drain. Stir in the chili, salsa and chilies. Bring to a boil. Reduce heat; simmer, uncovered, for 5 minutes.
2. Spoon about ½ cupful beef mixture off center on each tortilla. Top each with a slice of cheese; roll up. Serve with taco sauce and lettuce if desired.

❝These easy burritos are packed with a bean and beef filling for a delicious taste of the Southwest. And since the recipe makes eight big burritos, you can feed a crowd!❞

— JENNIFER MCKINNEY WASHINGTON, ILLINOIS

Meatballs Stroganoff

This is one of my most-loved recipes from my mother. It's a comfort food classic over egg noodles.

— **NANCY CARNES** CLEARWATER, MINNESOTA

PREP: 40 MIN.   **COOK:** 25 MIN.   **MAKES:** 4 SERVINGS

- 1 egg, lightly beaten
- ½ cup soft bread crumbs
- 2 tablespoons chopped onion
- ½ teaspoon celery salt
- ¼ teaspoon dried marjoram
- ⅛ teaspoon garlic salt
- ⅛ teaspoon pepper
- 1 pound ground beef
- 2 tablespoons all-purpose flour
- 1 tablespoon canola oil
- 1 can (10¾ ounces) condensed cream of mushroom soup, undiluted
- ¾ cup water
- ⅓ cup sour cream
  Hot cooked egg noodles

1. In a large bowl, combine the first seven ingredients. Crumble beef over mixture and mix well.

2. Place flour in a large shallow bowl; gently roll meatballs in flour. In a large skillet, brown meatballs in oil; drain. Combine soup and water; pour over meatballs. Bring to a boil. Reduce heat; cover and simmer for 20-25 minutes or until meat is no longer pink, stirring occasionally.

3. Stir in the sour cream; heat through (do not boil). Serve with egg noodles.

Mexi-Mac Skillet

PREP/TOTAL TIME: 30 MIN.   **MAKES:** 5 SERVINGS

- 1 pound lean ground beef (90% lean)
- 1 large onion, chopped
- 1 can (14½ ounces) diced tomatoes, undrained
- 1 can (8 ounces) tomato sauce
- 1 cup fresh or frozen corn
- ½ cup water
- 1¼ teaspoons chili powder
- 1 teaspoon dried oregano
- ½ teaspoon salt
- ⅔ cup uncooked elbow macaroni
- ⅔ cup shredded reduced-fat cheddar cheese

1. In a large nonstick skillet over medium-high heat, cook beef and onion until meat is no longer pink; drain. Stir in tomatoes, tomato sauce, corn, water, chili powder, oregano and salt.

2. Bring to a boil; stir in macaroni. Reduce heat; cover and cook 18-22 minutes or until macaroni is tender. Sprinkle with cheese.

> "This is the tastiest and quickest recipe I have in my files, and it's one of my husband's favorites. It really saves time because there's no need to precook the macaroni."
>
> — **MAURANE RAMSEY** FORT WAYNE, INDIANA

Stuffed Cabbage Rolls

In our area of Pennsylvania, cabbage rolls are frequently served at special occasions of all kinds. They can be stuffed with pork or other kinds of fillings. Though we've tried the others, my family always goes back to ground beef—it just tastes best to us.

— **JEAN PARSONS** SARVER, PENNSYLVANIA

PREP: 30 MIN. **COOK:** 1¼ HOURS **MAKES:** 4-6 SERVINGS

- 1 large head cabbage
- 1 cup quick-cooking rice, cooked and cooled
- 1 pound lean ground beef (90% lean)
- 1 medium onion, chopped
- 2 tablespoons Worcestershire sauce
- ½ teaspoon salt
- ¼ teaspoon pepper
- 1 can (10¾ ounces) condensed tomato soup, undiluted, divided
- ½ cup water

1. Cook cabbage in boiling water only until leaves fall off head. Reserve 14-16 large leaves for rolls; set aside remaining cabbage.
2. In a bowl, combine rice, beef, onion, Worcestershire sauce, salt, pepper and ¼ cup soup. Put 2 to 3 tablespoons meat mixture on each cabbage leaf. Fold in sides, then roll up leaves to completely enclose meat.
3. Line a Dutch oven with leftover cabbage leaves. Combine remaining soup and water; pour over cabbage. Stack cabbage rolls on top of sauce. Cover. Bring to a boil. Reduce heat; cover and simmer on low for 1 to 1½ hours or until rolls are tender.
4. Remove rolls and cabbage. If desired, sauce may be thickened by boiling over high heat. Spoon sauce over rolls and cabbage and serve immediately.

Ramen-Vegetable Beef Skillet

Here's a unique flavor combination in an easy skillet dinner. Using ramen noodles makes it affordable.

— **MARLENE MCALLISTER** PORTLAND, MICHIGAN

PREP/TOTAL TIME: 30 MIN. **MAKES:** 4 SERVINGS

- 1 pound ground beef
- 1½ cups sliced fresh carrots
- ¾ cup sliced onion
- 1 cup water
- 1 cup shredded cabbage
- 1 cup sliced fresh mushrooms
- 1 cup chopped green pepper
- 3 tablespoons soy sauce
- 1 package (3 ounces) beef ramen noodles

1. In a large skillet, cook the beef, carrots and onion over medium heat until meat is no longer pink and carrots are crisp-tender; drain.
2. Add the water, cabbage, mushrooms, green pepper, soy sauce and the contents of seasoning packet from the noodles. Break noodles into small pieces; add to pan. Cover and cook for 10 minutes or until liquid is absorbed and noodles are tender.

top tip Ground beef may be labeled with the cut of meat that it was ground from (such as ground chuck, round or sirloin). It may also be labeled according to its fat content (such as 80% or 90% lean).

Beef Fettuccine Dinner

PREP/TOTAL TIME: 20 MIN.
MAKES: 4 SERVINGS

- 1 **pound ground beef**
- 1½ **cups water**
- 1 **package (4.3 ounces) fettuccine and beef-flavored sauce mix**
- 1 **can (8 ounces) tomato sauce**
- 2 **teaspoons chili powder**
- 1 **can (11 ounces) whole kernel corn, drained**
- 1 **cup (4 ounces) shredded cheddar cheese, divided**

1. In a large skillet, cook beef over medium heat until no longer pink; drain. Add water; bring to a boil. Stir in the fettuccine mix, tomato sauce and chili powder. Return to a boil. Reduce heat; simmer, uncovered, for 7 minutes or until thickened.

2. Stir in corn and ⅔ cup cheese; heat through. Sprinkle with remaining cheese.

Pizza Spaghetti

The idea for this recipe came to me when I saw someone dip a slice of pizza into a pasta dish. My wife and kids love it and so do my friends!

— **ROBERT SMITH** LAS VEGAS, NEVADA

PREP: 20 MIN. **COOK:** 30 MIN.
MAKES: 6 SERVINGS

- ½ **pound lean ground beef (90% lean)**
- ½ **pound Italian turkey sausage links, casings removed, crumbled**
- ½ **cup chopped sweet onion**
- 4 **cans (8 ounces each) no-salt-added tomato sauce**
- 3 **ounces sliced turkey pepperoni**
- 1 **tablespoon sugar**
- 2 **teaspoons minced fresh parsley or ½ teaspoon dried parsley flakes**
- 2 **teaspoons minced fresh basil or ½ teaspoon dried basil**
- 9 **ounces uncooked whole wheat spaghetti**
- 3 **tablespoons grated Parmesan cheese**

1. In a large nonstick skillet, cook the beef, sausage and onion over medium heat until meat is no longer pink; drain.

2. Stir in the tomato sauce, pepperoni, sugar, parsley and basil. Bring to a boil. Reduce heat; simmer, uncovered, for 20-25 minutes or until thickened. Meanwhile, cook spaghetti according to package directions.

3. Drain spaghetti; toss with sauce. Sprinkle with cheese.

Since I don't get home from work until dinnertime, I need something fast. This is perfect because it's so easy. I fix it twice a month and never have any leftovers.
— **BARBARA SPOHN** BROKEN ARROW, OKLAHOMA

BEEF FETTUCCINE DINNER

Easy Cuban Picadillo

PREP/TOTAL TIME: 30 MIN.
MAKES: 4 SERVINGS

- 1 pound lean ground beef (90% lean)
- 1 small green pepper, chopped
- ¼ cup chopped onion
- 1 can (8 ounces) tomato sauce
- ½ cup sliced pimiento-stuffed olives
- ¼ cup raisins
- 1 tablespoon cider vinegar
- 2 cups hot cooked rice

1. In a large nonstick skillet, cook the beef, pepper and onion over medium heat until meat is no longer pink; drain.
2. Stir in the tomato sauce, olives, raisins and vinegar. Cook for 5-6 minutes or until raisins are plumped. Serve with rice.

❝A friend gave me this delicious recipe years ago. I've made it ever since for family and friends, and they all love it. My daughter says it's the best dish I make and likes to take leftovers to school for lunch the next day.❞
— MARIE WIELGUS WAYNE, NEW JERSEY

Stovetop Meat Loaves

Who says meat loaf has to bake in the oven for hours? For this convenient recipe, all you need is your stovetop and 30 minutes. It's a fast and easy recipe to make for one or two people.
— **EMILY SUND** GENESEO, ILLINOIS

PREP/TOTAL TIME: 30 MIN. **MAKES:** 2 SERVINGS

- 3 tablespoons 2% milk
- 2 tablespoons quick-cooking oats
- 1 tablespoon chopped onion
- ¼ teaspoon salt
- ½ pound lean ground beef
- ½ teaspoon cornstarch
- ½ cup Italian tomato sauce
- ¼ cup cold water

1. In a small bowl, combine the milk, oats, onion and salt. Crumble beef over mixture and mix well. Shape into two loaves.
2. In a small nonstick skillet, brown loaves on all sides; drain. Combine the cornstarch, tomato sauce and water until smooth. Pour over meat loaves. Bring to a boil. Reduce heat to medium-low; cover and cook for 15-20 minutes or until meat is no longer pink.

Hamburger Stir-Fry

Here's a quick, easy teriyaki stir-fry that uses hamburger instead of the traditional beef strips. It has a nice sauce and is different enough to be a treat for the taste buds.

— **KATHIE AND JOHN HORST** WESTFIELD, NEW YORK

PREP/TOTAL TIME: 25 MIN. **MAKES:** 4 SERVINGS

- 1 **tablespoon sugar**
- 1 **tablespoon cornstarch**
- 1 **tablespoon ground mustard**
- ⅓ **cup water**
- ⅓ **cup reduced-sodium teriyaki sauce**
- 1 **pound lean ground beef (90% lean)**
- 1 **package (16 ounces) frozen asparagus stir-fry vegetable blend**
- 1 **medium onion, halved and thinly sliced**
- 2 **teaspoons canola oil**
- 2 **cups hot cooked rice**
- 2 **teaspoons sesame seeds**

1. In a small bowl, combine the sugar, cornstarch and mustard. Stir in water and teriyaki sauce until smooth; set aside.

2. In a large skillet or wok, stir-fry beef until no longer pink; drain and set aside. In the same pan, stir-fry the vegetable blend and onion in oil until crisp-tender.

3. Stir cornstarch mixture and add to the pan. Bring to a boil; cook and stir for 1-2 minutes or until thickened. Add beef; heat through. Serve with rice. Sprinkle with sesame seeds.

Inside-Out Cabbage Rolls

PREP: 15 MIN. **COOK:** 30 MIN. **MAKES:** 6 SERVINGS

- 1 **pound lean ground beef (90% lean)**
- 1 **large onion, chopped**
- 1 **large green pepper, chopped**
- 1 **small head cabbage, chopped**
- 1 **can (10 ounces) diced tomatoes and green chilies**
- 1 **cup reduced-sodium beef broth**
- 1 **can (8 ounces) pizza sauce**
- 1 **cup cooked brown rice**
- ½ **cup shredded reduced-fat cheddar cheese**

1. In a Dutch oven, cook the beef, onion and green pepper over medium heat until meat is no longer pink; drain.

2. Stir in the cabbage, tomatoes, broth and pizza sauce. Bring to a boil. Reduce heat; cover and simmer for 20-25 minutes or until cabbage is tender, stirring occasionally.

3. Stir in rice; heat through. Remove from the heat. Sprinkle with cheese; cover and let stand until cheese is melted.

❝Here's a hearty one-dish meal that's lower in fat but very filling. The cabbage, ground beef and brown rice give it a comforting down-home feel.❞

— **LISA WILLIAMS** COMSTOCK PARK, MICHIGAN

STOVETOP SUPPERS

Dress up store-bought ravioli and make it really special—prosciutto and mozzarella help to do the trick.

— **TASTE OF HOME TEST KITCHEN**

PRESTO RAVIOLI

Presto Ravioli

PREP/TOTAL TIME: 30 MIN.
MAKES: 4 SERVINGS

- **1 pound ground beef**
- **¾ cup chopped green pepper**
- **1 ounce prosciutto or deli ham, chopped**
- **3 cups spaghetti sauce**
- **¾ cup water**
- **1 package (25 ounces) frozen cheese ravioli**
- **1 cup (4 ounces) shredded part-skim mozzarella cheese**

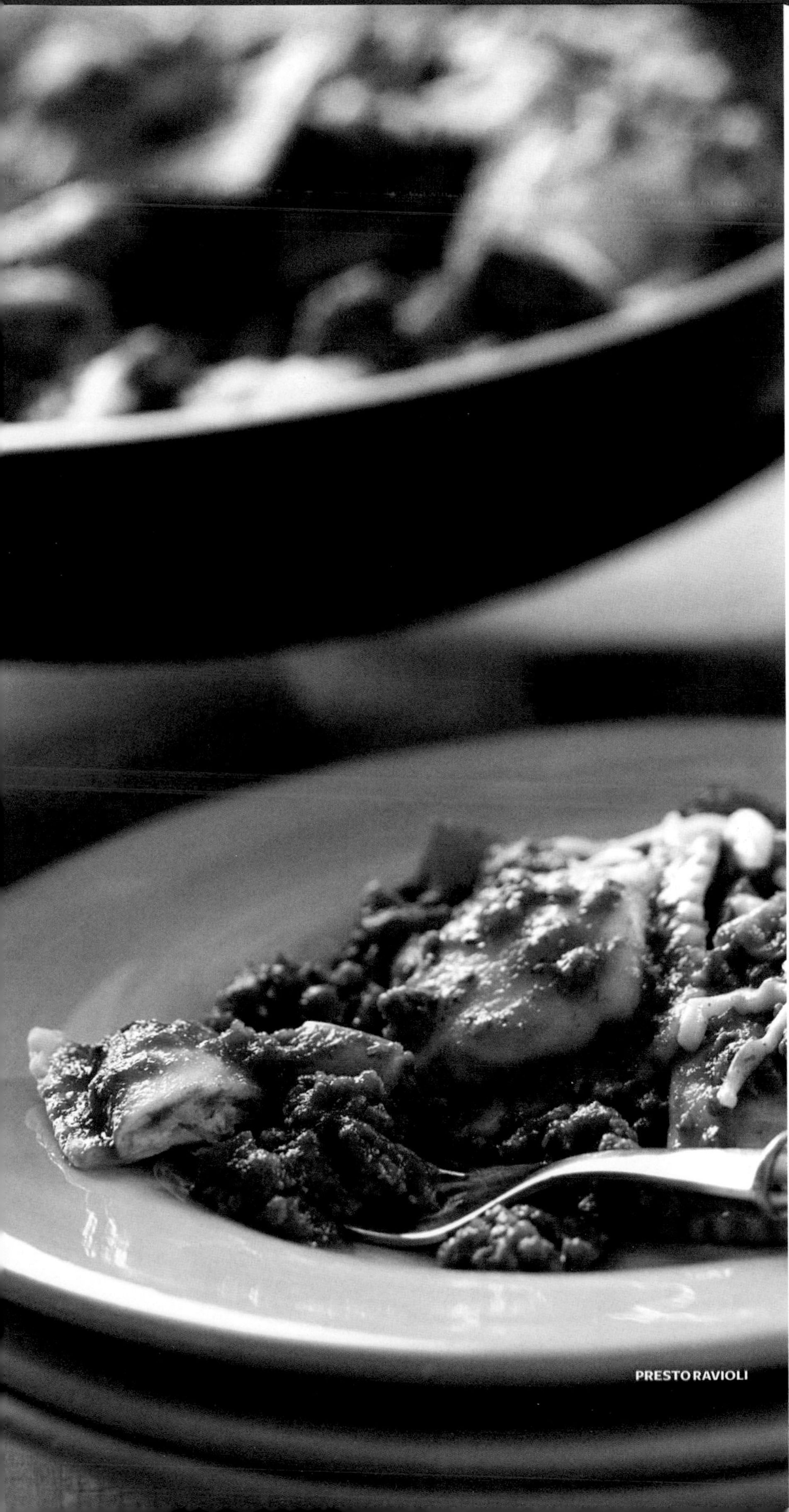

1. In a large skillet, cook the beef, green pepper and prosciutto over medium heat until beef is no longer pink; drain.
2. Stir in spaghetti sauce and water; bring to a boil. Add ravioli. Reduce heat; cover and simmer for 7-9 minutes or until ravioli is tender, stirring once. Sprinkle with cheese. Simmer, uncovered, 1-2 minutes longer or until cheese is melted.

Skillet Shepherd's Pie

This is the best shepherd's pie I've ever tasted. It's very quick to make, and I usually have most of the ingredients already on hand. Round out the meal with fresh fruit.

— **TIRZAH SANDT** SAN DIEGO, CALIFORNIA

PREP/TOTAL TIME: 30 MIN.
MAKES: 6 SERVINGS

- **1 pound ground beef**
- **1 cup chopped onion**
- **2 cups frozen corn, thawed**
- **2 cups frozen peas, thawed**
- **2 tablespoons ketchup**
- **1 tablespoon Worcestershire sauce**
- **2 teaspoons minced garlic**
- **1 tablespoon cornstarch**
- **1 teaspoon beef bouillon granules**
- **½ cup cold water**
- **½ cup sour cream**
- **3½ cups mashed potatoes (prepared with milk and butter)**
- **¾ cup shredded cheddar cheese**

1. In a large skillet, cook beef and onion over medium heat until meat is no longer pink; drain. Stir in the corn, peas, ketchup, Worcestershire sauce and garlic. Reduce heat; cover and cook for 5 minutes.
2. Combine the cornstarch, bouillon and water until well blended; stir into beef mixture. Bring to a boil; cook and stir for 2 minutes or until thickened. Stir in sour cream and heat through (do not boil).
3. Spread mashed potatoes over the top; sprinkle with cheese. Cover and cook until potatoes are heated through and the cheese is melted.

Beef Taco Skillet

PREP/TOTAL TIME: 20 MIN.
MAKES: 6 SERVINGS

- 1 **pound ground beef**
- 1 **small red onion, chopped**
- 1 **can (15¼ ounces) whole kernel corn, drained**
- 10 **corn tortillas (6 inches), cut into 1-inch pieces**
- 1 **bottle (8 ounces) taco sauce**
- 1¼ **cups shredded cheddar cheese, divided**
  Hot pepper sauce, optional

In a large skillet, cook beef and onion over medium heat until meat is no longer pink; drain. Add the corn, tortillas, taco sauce and 1 cup cheese; heat through. Sprinkle with remaining cheese. Serve with pepper sauce if desired.

Hawaiian Beef

My dad, who still enjoys experimenting in the kitchen, created this elegant dish when I was a little girl. Sometimes I prepare it the day before and warm it up while I'm cooking the rice.

— **MARILYN TAUS** MISSISSAUGA, ONTARIO

PREP/TOTAL TIME: 25 MIN.
MAKES: 2 SERVINGS

- ½ **pound lean ground beef (90% lean)**
- 1 **medium onion, halved and sliced**
- ⅓ **cup sliced celery**
- ⅓ **cup chopped green pepper**
- 1 **garlic clove, minced**
- 2 **teaspoons butter**
- 1 **can (8 ounces) unsweetened pineapple chunks**
- ¼ **cup packed brown sugar**
- 1 **tablespoon all-purpose flour**
- 1 **tablespoon white wine vinegar**
- ¼ **teaspoon salt**
- 1 **cup hot cooked rice**

1. In a small skillet, cook beef over medium heat until no longer pink; drain and set aside. In the same skillet, saute the onion, celery, green pepper and garlic in butter until crisp-tender.

2. Drain pineapple, reserving juice; set pineapple aside. Add enough water to the juice to measure ½ cup. In a bowl, combine the brown sugar, flour, vinegar, salt and pineapple juice mixture until smooth. Add to skillet.

3. Bring to a boil; cook and stir for 2 minutes or until thickened. Stir in the beef and pineapple; heat through. Serve with rice.

Busy day? Save time and money with a stovetop supper the whole family will love. It calls for handy convenience products, so it can be on the table in minutes.

— **KELLY RODER** FAIRFAX, VIRGINIA

BEEF TACO SKILLET

73

70

63

Casseroles
& Oven Entrees

Pizza Tot Casserole

PREP: 10 MIN. **BAKE:** 30 MIN.
MAKES: 8 SERVINGS

- 1½ pounds ground beef
- 1 medium green pepper, chopped, optional
- 1 medium onion, chopped
- ½ pound sliced fresh mushrooms
- 1 can (15 ounces) pizza sauce
- 1 teaspoon dried basil
- 3 cups (12 ounces) shredded part-skim mozzarella cheese
- 1 package (32 ounces) frozen Tater Tots
- 1 cup (4 ounces) shredded cheddar cheese

1. In a large skillet, cook the beef, green pepper, onion and mushrooms over medium heat until meat is no longer pink; drain. Add pizza sauce and basil.

2. Transfer to a greased 3-qt. baking dish. Top with mozzarella cheese and potatoes. Bake, uncovered, at 400° for 30-35 minutes or until potatoes are lightly browned.

3. Sprinkle with cheddar cheese; bake 5 minutes longer or until cheese is melted.

French Meat Pie

Some time ago, a co-worker brought a meat pie for lunch. The aroma was familiar to me, and I asked for a taste. To my amazement, it was the same pie my grandmother used to serve when I was a youngster! I copied the recipe, and have been enjoying French Meat Pie ever since. It's still delicious!

— **RITA WINTERBERGER** HUSON, MONTANA

PREP: 20 MIN. **BAKE:** 30 MIN.
MAKES: 6-8 SERVINGS

- 1 pound ground beef
- 1 pound ground pork
- 1 large onion, thinly sliced
- 1 cup mashed potatoes
- 2 teaspoons ground allspice
- 1 teaspoon salt
- ¼ teaspoon pepper
  Pastry for double-crust pie (9 inches)
- 1 egg, beaten, optional

1. In a Dutch oven, cook the beef, pork and onion over medium heat until meat is no longer pink; drain.

2. In a small bowl, combine potatoes and seasonings. Roll out half of pastry to fit a 9-in. pie plate; trim pastry even with edge of plate. Fill with meat mixture.

3. Roll out remaining pastry to fit top of pie; place over filling. Trim, seal and flute edges. Cut slits in pastry. Brush with egg if desired. Bake at 375° for 30-35 minutes or until golden brown.

For a spin on a classic casserole, try my easy version. For a fun twist, just add your family's favorite pizza toppings!

— **SHARON SKILDUM** MAPLE GROVE, MINNESOTA

PIZZA TOT CASSEROLE

Meat Loaf Wellington

I took what I liked from a few different recipes and came up with this rich and cheesy loaf with golden brown crust. I make it for neighbors or friends who are sick or need help. It's great comfort food!

— **JANINE TALBOT** SANTAQUIN, UTAH

PREP: 20 MIN. **BAKE:** 1¼ HOURS
MAKES: 8 SERVINGS

- 1 **egg, lightly beaten**
- 1 **cup spaghetti sauce, divided**
- ¼ **cup dry bread crumbs**
- ½ **teaspoon salt**
- ¼ **teaspoon pepper**
- 1½ **pounds ground beef**
- 2 **cups (8 ounces) shredded part-skim mozzarella cheese, divided**
- 1 **tablespoon minced fresh parsley**
- 1 **tube (8 ounces) refrigerated crescent rolls**

1. In a large bowl, combine the egg, ⅓ cup spaghetti sauce, bread crumbs, salt and pepper. Crumble beef over mixture and mix well.

2. On a piece of heavy-duty foil, pat beef mixture into a 12-in. x 8-in. rectangle. Sprinkle 1 cup cheese and the parsley to within 1 in. of edges. Roll up jelly-roll style, starting with a long side and peeling foil away while rolling. Seal seam and ends. Place seam side down in a greased 13-in. x 9-in. baking dish.

3. Bake, uncovered, at 350° for 1 hour; drain. Unroll crescent dough; seal seams and perforations. Drape dough over meat loaf to cover top, sides and ends; seal ends. Bake for 14-18 minutes or until a thermometer reads 160° and crust is golden brown. Sprinkle with remaining cheese; bake 1 minute longer. Let stand for 5 minutes.

4. Using two large spatulas, carefully transfer to a serving platter. Serve with remaining spaghetti sauce.

Cheeseburger Pockets

PREP: 30 MIN. **BAKE:** 10 MIN. **MAKES:** 5 SERVINGS

- ½ **pound ground beef**
- 1 **tablespoon chopped onion**
- ½ **teaspoon salt**
- ⅛ **teaspoon pepper**
- 1 **tube (12 ounces) refrigerated buttermilk biscuits**
- 5 **slices process American cheese**

1. In a large skillet, cook the beef, onion, salt and pepper over medium heat until meat is no longer pink; drain and cool.

2. Place two biscuits overlapping on a floured surface; roll out into a 5-in. oval. Place about ¼ cup of meat mixture on one side. Fold a cheese slice to fit over meat mixture. Fold dough over filling; press edges with a fork to seal. Repeat with remaining biscuits, meat mixture and cheese.

3. Place on a greased baking sheet. Prick tops with a fork. Bake at 400° for 10 minutes or until golden brown.

“Ground beef is my favorite meat to cook with because it's so versatile and economical. Refrigerated biscuits save the trouble of making dough from scratch.”

— **PAT CHAMBLESS** CROWDER, OKLAHOMA

Beef & Tater Bake

PREP: 25 MIN. **BAKE:** 25 MIN. **MAKES:** 12 SERVINGS

- 4 **cups frozen Tater Tots**
- 1 **pound ground beef**
- 1 **package (16 ounces) frozen chopped broccoli, thawed**
- 1 **can (10¾ ounces) condensed cream of broccoli soup, undiluted**
- 1 **medium tomato, chopped**
- 1 **can (2.8 ounces) French-fried onions, divided**
- 1 **cup (4 ounces) shredded Colby-Monterey Jack cheese, divided**
- ⅓ **cup 2% milk**
- ¼ **teaspoon garlic powder**
- ⅛ **teaspoon pepper**

1. Place Tater Tots in an ungreased 13-in. x 9-in. baking dish. Bake, uncovered, at 400° for 10 minutes.
2. Meanwhile, in a large skillet, cook beef over medium heat until no longer pink; drain. Stir in the broccoli, soup, tomato, ¾ cup French-fried onions, ½ cup cheese, milk, garlic powder and pepper; heat through. Pour over Tater Tots.
3. Cover and bake for 20 minutes. Uncover; sprinkle with remaining onions and cheese. Bake 5-10 minutes longer or until cheese is melted.

❝The entire family will enjoy this heartwarming all-in-one dinner. Plus, it offers easy cleanup!❞
— **MIKE TCHOU** PEPPER PIKE, OHIO

Spaghetti Pizza Casserole

I first tried this great-tasting dish at an office Christmas party, where it quickly became everyone's favorite. It's a wonderful alternative to ordinary spaghetti. If you prefer, use 2 beaten eggs instead of the egg substitute.
— **KIM NEER** KALAMAZOO, MICHIGAN

PREP: 25 MIN. **BAKE:** 25 MIN. **MAKES:** 9 SERVINGS

- 1 **package (7 ounces) spaghetti**
- ½ **cup egg substitute**
- ¼ **cup grated Parmesan cheese**
- 1 **pound lean ground beef (90% lean)**
- 1 **medium onion, chopped**
- ½ **cup chopped green pepper**
- ½ **cup chopped sweet yellow pepper**
- 2 **garlic cloves, minced**
- 1 **jar (24 ounces) spaghetti sauce**
- 1 **teaspoon Italian seasoning**
- 1 **teaspoon dried basil**
- ½ **teaspoon salt**
- ¼ **teaspoon pepper**
- ½ **pound sliced fresh mushrooms**
- 1½ **cups (6 ounces) shredded part-skim mozzarella cheese**

1. Cook spaghetti according to package directions. Drain and rinse with cold water. In a large bowl, toss spaghetti with egg substitute and Parmesan cheese. Spread evenly into a 15-in. x 10-in. x 1-in. baking pan coated with cooking spray; set aside.
2. In a large nonstick skillet, cook the beef, onion and peppers over medium heat until meat is no longer pink; drain. Add garlic; cook 1 minute longer. Stir in spaghetti sauce and seasonings; heat through.
3. Spoon over spaghetti. Top with mushrooms and mozzarella cheese. Bake, uncovered, at 350° for 25-30 minutes or until lightly browned. Let stand for 5 minutes before serving.

Tortillas replace lasagna noodles in an easy casserole with big south-of-the-border taste. With beef, refried beans, salsa, enchilada sauce, chilies and cheese, it's a fiesta of flavors.

— **TINA NEWHAUSER** PETERBOROUGH, NEW HAMPSHIRE

Favorite Mexican Lasagna

PREP: 25 MIN. **BAKE:** 40 MIN. + STANDING
MAKES: 12 SERVINGS

- 1¼ **pounds ground beef**
- 1 **medium onion, chopped**
- 4 **garlic cloves, minced**
- 2 **cups salsa**
- 1 **can (16 ounces) refried beans**
- 1 **can (15 ounces) black beans, rinsed and drained**
- 1 **can (10 ounces) enchilada sauce**
- 1 **can (4 ounces) chopped green chilies**
- 1 **envelope taco seasoning**
- ¼ **teaspoon pepper**
- 6 **flour tortillas (10 inches)**
- 3 **cups (12 ounces) shredded Mexican cheese blend, divided**
- 2 **cups crushed tortilla chips**
  Sliced ripe olives, guacamole, chopped tomatoes and sour cream, optional

1. In a large skillet, cook beef and onion over medium heat until meat is no longer pink. Add garlic; cook 1 minute longer. Drain. Stir in the salsa, beans, enchilada sauce, chilies, taco seasoning and pepper; heat through.

2. Spread 1 cup meat mixture in a greased 13-in. x 9-in. baking dish. Layer with two tortillas, a third of the remaining meat mixture and 1 cup cheese. Repeat the layers. Top with remaining tortillas and meat mixture.

3. Cover and bake at 375° for 30 minutes. Uncover; sprinkle with remaining cheese and top with tortilla chips.

4. Bake 10-15 minutes longer or until cheese is melted. Let stand for 10 minutes before cutting. Serve with the toppings of your choice.

top tip

Tortillas make a great pie crust in a pinch. Spray a pie plate with cooking spray, then drop in a 10-inch flour tortilla. Add your pie filling and bake as usual. This lifesaver works great with savory meat pies.

—**MARIAN D.**
SPANAWAY, WASHINGTON

FAVORITE MEXICAN LASAGNA

Unstuffed Peppers

PREP/TOTAL TIME: 30 MIN.
MAKES: 6 SERVINGS

- 1 cup uncooked instant rice
- 1 pound ground beef
- 2 medium green peppers, cut into 1-inch pieces
- ½ cup chopped onion
- 1 jar (26 ounces) marinara sauce
- 1½ teaspoons salt-free seasoning blend
- ½ cup shredded Italian cheese blend
- ½ cup seasoned bread crumbs
- 1 tablespoon olive oil

1. Cook rice according to package directions. Meanwhile, in a large skillet, cook the beef, green peppers and onion over medium-high heat until meat is no longer pink; drain. Stir in the rice, marinara sauce and seasoning blend. Stir in cheese.

2. Transfer to a greased 2-qt. baking dish. Toss bread crumbs and oil; sprinkle over the top. Bake at 350° for 8-10 minutes or until heated through and topping is golden brown.

Hamburger Potpie

A must-try for the meat-and-potato lover in your home, slices of this hearty meal in one are sure to satisfy. Best of all, a refrigerated pastry crust makes it easy as pie.
— **TASTE OF HOME TEST KITCHEN**

PREP: 25 MIN. **BAKE:** 30 MIN. + STANDING
MAKES: 6 SERVINGS

- 1 pound lean ground beef (90% lean)
- 2 medium onions, chopped
- 1½ cups finely chopped carrots
- 2 cups mashed potatoes (without added milk and butter)
- ¼ cup beef broth
- 1 teaspoon rubbed sage
- ¾ teaspoon salt
- ½ teaspoon dried thyme
- ½ teaspoon dried marjoram
- ½ teaspoon pepper
- 1 sheet refrigerated pie pastry

1. In a large nonstick skillet, cook the beef, onions and carrots over medium heat until meat is no longer pink; drain if necessary. Stir in the potatoes, broth and seasonings. Spoon into an ungreased 9-in. pie plate.

2. Place pastry over filling; crimp the edges to seal. Cut slits in top. Bake at 400° for 30-35 minutes or until crust is golden brown. Let potpie stand for 10 minutes before cutting.

If you like stuffed peppers, you will love a speedy version that's ready in just half an hour. Instead of cooking the instant rice, you can use 2 cups of leftover cooked rice if you have it on hand.
— **BETH DEWYER** DU BOIS, PENNSYLVANIA

UNSTUFFED PEPPERS

Kellee's Nacho Noodles

PREP: 25 MIN. **BAKE:** 15 MIN. **MAKES:** 4 SERVINGS

- 2 cups uncooked egg noodles
- 1 pound ground beef
- 1 can (14½ ounces) diced tomatoes, undrained
- 1 can (10¾ ounces) condensed nacho cheese soup, undiluted
- 1 jar (5¾ ounces) sliced pimiento-stuffed olives, drained
- 1 can (4 ounces) chopped green chilies
- 1½ cups (6 ounces) shredded cheddar cheese
- 2 cups crushed tortilla chips
- ⅓ cup prepared ranch salad dressing
  Shredded lettuce, sour cream and/or salsa, optional

1. Cook noodles according to package directions; drain. Meanwhile, in a large saucepan, cook beef over medium heat until no longer pink; drain. Stir in the tomatoes, soup, olives and chilies. Bring to a boil. Reduce heat; simmer, uncovered, for 10 minutes. Stir in noodles.

2. Transfer to a greased 11-in. x 7-in. baking dish. Sprinkle with cheese. Bake at 350° for 15-20 minutes or until heated through. Top with tortilla chips; drizzle with salad dressing. Serve with lettuce, sour cream and/or salsa if desired.

66 **My daughter came up with this recipe when she was visiting her fiance's family. After sampling it, her future father-in-law thought she was a pretty good cook!** 99

— **KENDRA MCINTYRE** WEBSTER, SOUTH DAKOTA

Italian Pinwheel Meat Loaf

I have been making my special meat loaf for decades. The cheesy filling and saucy topping make it impossible to resist. I assemble it early in the day and just pop it into the oven when I'm ready.

— **GAIL BUSS** BEVERLY HILLS, FLORIDA

PREP: 25 MIN. **BAKE:** 1¼ HOURS + STANDING **MAKES:** 8 SERVINGS

- 2 eggs, lightly beaten
- ¾ cup seasoned bread crumbs
- ½ cup spaghetti sauce or ketchup
- 1 tablespoon minced fresh parsley
- 1 garlic clove, minced
- ½ teaspoon dried oregano
- ¼ teaspoon onion powder
- ¼ teaspoon salt
- ¼ teaspoon pepper
- 2 pounds lean ground beef (90% lean)
- 16 slices part-skim mozzarella cheese, divided
- ¼ pound thinly sliced deli ham
  Additional spaghetti sauce, warmed, optional

1. In a large bowl, combine the first nine ingredients. Crumble beef over mixture and mix well.

2. On a piece of heavy-duty foil, pat beef mixture into a 12-in. x 10-in. rectangle. Layer with six cheese slices, ham and six more cheese slices.

3. Roll up jelly roll-style, starting with a short side and peeling foil away while rolling. Seal seam and ends. Place seam side down in a greased 13-in. x 9-in. baking dish.

4. Bake, uncovered, at 350° for 70 minutes or until no pink remains and a thermometer reads 160°. Top with remaining cheese; bake 5 minutes longer or until cheese is melted. Let stand for 10 minutes before slicing. Serve with additional spaghetti sauce if desired.

Old-Fashioned Cabbage Rolls

PREP: 25 MIN. **BAKE:** 1½ HOURS **MAKES:** 6 SERVINGS

- 1 medium head cabbage (3 pounds)
- ½ pound uncooked ground beef
- ½ pound uncooked ground pork
- 1 can (15 ounces) tomato sauce, divided
- 1 small onion, chopped
- ½ cup uncooked long grain rice
- 1 tablespoon dried parsley flakes
- ½ teaspoon salt
- ½ teaspoon snipped fresh dill or dill weed
- ⅛ teaspoon cayenne pepper
- 1 can (14½ ounces) diced tomatoes, undrained
- ½ teaspoon sugar

1. Cook cabbage in boiling water just until outer leaves pull away easily from head. Set aside 12 large leaves for rolls. In a small bowl, combine the beef, pork, ½ cup tomato sauce, onion, rice, parsley, salt, dill and cayenne; mix well.

2. Cut out the thick vein from the bottom of each leaf, making a V-shaped cut. Place about ¼ cup meat mixture on a cabbage leaf; overlap cut ends of leaf. Fold in sides. Beginning from the cut end, roll up. Repeat.

3. Slice the remaining cabbage; place in an ovenproof Dutch oven. Arrange the cabbage rolls seam side down over sliced cabbage. Combine the tomatoes, sugar and remaining tomato sauce; pour over the rolls.

4. Cover and bake at 350° for 1½ hours or until cabbage rolls are tender.

> ❝It was an abundance of dill in my garden that led me to try this recipe. My family liked the taste so much that from then on, I made my cabbage rolls with a hint of dill.❞

— **FLORENCE KRANTZ** BISMARCK, NORTH DAKOTA

Cheddar-Olive Meat Loaf

Swirled with a rich and flavorful sour cream filling, my mother's meat loaf is something special. It's a timeless centerpiece for Sunday dinner or even a festive occasion.

— **SUSAN HANSEN** AUBURN, ALABAMA

PREP: 35 MIN. **BAKE:** 65 MIN. + STANDING
MAKES: 6 SERVINGS

- ½ cup milk
- 2 eggs, lightly beaten
- 1 tablespoon Worcestershire sauce
- 1 cup crushed cornflakes
- ½ cup finely chopped onion
- 3 tablespoons finely chopped celery
- 1 teaspoon salt
- ½ teaspoon ground mustard
- ½ teaspoon rubbed sage
- ¼ teaspoon pepper
- 1½ pounds ground beef
- 1 cup (8 ounces) sour cream
- 1 cup (4 ounces) finely shredded cheddar cheese
- ½ cup sliced pimiento-stuffed olives

1. In a large bowl, combine the first 10 ingredients. Crumble beef over mixture and mix well.

2. On a large piece of foil, pat beef mixture into a 14-in. x 10-in. rectangle. Spread sour cream to within ½ in. of edges. Sprinkle with the cheese and olives.

3. Roll up meat loaf, jelly-roll style, starting with a short side and peeling away foil while rolling. Seal seam and ends. Place seam side down in a greased 13-in. x 9-in. baking dish.

4. Bake, uncovered, at 350° for 65-75 minutes or until meat is no longer pink and a thermometer reads 160°. Let stand for 10 minutes before slicing.

Give Jack Frost the cold shoulder by setting a comforting hot dish on the table. This hearty meal satisfies the biggest of appetites. Enjoy one casserole and freeze the other, or serve them both when entertaining.

— **JOY SAUERS** SIOUX FALLS, SOUTH DAKOTA

Hearty Macaroni Casserole

PREP: 20 MIN. **BAKE:** 30 MIN.
MAKES: 2 CASSEROLES (4 SERVINGS EACH)

- 1 package (7¼ ounces) macaroni and cheese dinner mix
- 1 pound ground beef
- 1 cup chopped green pepper
- ½ cup chopped onion
- 1 can (14½ ounces) Italian diced tomatoes, drained
- 2 cups (8 ounces) shredded cheddar cheese, divided
- 1 cup French-fried onions

1. Prepare macaroni and cheese according to package directions. Meanwhile, in a large skillet, cook the beef, green pepper and onion over medium heat until meat is no longer pink; drain. Add to prepared macaroni. Stir in tomatoes.

2. Divide half of mixture between two greased 1½-qt. baking dishes; sprinkle each with ½ cup cheese. Top with remaining mixture.

3. Sprinkle remaining cheese over one casserole. Cover and freeze for up to 3 months. Sprinkle the second casserole with French-fried onions. Bake, uncovered, at 350° for 30 minutes or until heated through.

To use frozen casserole: *Completely thaw in the refrigerator. Remove from the refrigerator 30 minutes before baking. Bake as directed.*

 top tip For best results, cover the casserole you plan to freeze with both plastic wrap and foil. Label and date the dish and include an expiration date. Most casseroles can be frozen for up to 3 months.

HEARTY MACARONI CASSEROLE

Individual Greek Pizzas

Here's a fresh and easy take on pizza that's loaded with big Mediterranean flavors. Friends and family will love these little single-serve pies.

— **TASTE OF HOME TEST KITCHEN**

PREP/TOTAL TIME: 30 MIN. **MAKES:** 4 SERVINGS

- 1 **package (6 ounces) fresh baby spinach**
- 1 **tablespoon olive oil**
- ½ **pound lean ground beef (90% lean)**
- 1 **can (15 ounces) pizza sauce**
- 4 **prebaked mini pizza crusts**
- 4 **plum tomatoes, sliced**
- 1 **cup crumbled tomato and basil feta cheese**
- ¼ **cup pine nuts, toasted**

1. In a large skillet, saute spinach in oil for 2-3 minutes or until wilted. Remove and set aside. In the same skillet, cook beef over medium heat until no longer pink; drain. Stir in pizza sauce; cook for 5 minutes or until heated through.

2. Place crusts in an ungreased 15-in. x 10-in. x 1-in. baking pan; spread with meat sauce to within ½ in. of edges. Layer with spinach, tomatoes, cheese and pine nuts. Bake at 450° for 8-10 minutes or until heated through.

Texas Cheeseburger

Your family will get a kick out of being served this giant cheeseburger. To cut down on last-minute preparation, bake the bun ahead and store it in an airtight container. Split the bun in half just before serving.

— **VICTORIA BECKHAM** HURST, TEXAS

PREP: 40 MIN. + CHILLING **BAKE:** 30 MIN. **MAKES:** 6 SERVINGS

- 1 **package (¼ ounces) active dry yeast**
- 1 **cup warm water (110° to 115°)**
- 1 **cup quick-cooking oats**
- ¼ **cup butter, softened**
- ¼ **cup instant nonfat dry milk powder**
- 1 **egg, separated**
- 2 **tablespoons sugar**
- 1 **teaspoon salt**
- 2¾ to 3¼ **cups all-purpose flour**
- 2 **tablespoons sesame seeds**

BURGER
- 1 **egg, beaten**
- ¾ **cup ketchup**
- ¾ **cup quick-cooking oats**
- 1 **teaspoon salt**
- 1½ **pounds ground beef**
     Lettuce leaves
- 4 **slices process American cheese**

1. In a large bowl, dissolve yeast in water. Add the oats, butter, milk powder, egg yolk, sugar, salt and 1 cup of flour; beat until smooth. Add enough remaining flour to form a stiff dough. Turn onto a floured surface; knead until smooth and elastic, about 6-8 minutes. Place in a greased bowl, turning once to grease the top. Cover and refrigerate for 8 hours or overnight. Cover and refrigerate egg white.

2. Punch dough down and shape into a ball. Press into a greased 9-in. round baking pan. Cover and let rise in a warm place until nearly doubled, about 45 minutes. Brush with egg white; sprinkle with sesame seeds. Bake at 350° for 30 minutes or until golden brown. Remove from pan to a wire rack to cool.

3. Combine the first four burger ingredients; crumble beef over mixture and mix well. On a greased broiler pan, shape meat mixture into an 8½-in. patty.

4. Bake, uncovered, at 350° for 30 minutes or until a thermometer reads 160°. To serve, split bun in half. Place lettuce, burger and cheese on bun bottom; replace top. Cut into wedges.

Zucchini Boats

After working hard all our lives and raising a family, we're now enjoying a simpler life. That back-to-the-basics approach includes old-fashioned comfort foods like this.
— **MRS. C. THON** ATLIN, BRITISH COLUMBIA

PREP: 35 MIN. **BAKE:** 25 MIN. **MAKES:** 4 SERVINGS

- 2 medium zucchini (about 8 inches)
- ¾ pound ground beef
- 1 small onion, chopped
- ½ cup chopped fresh mushrooms
- ½ cup chopped sweet red pepper
- ½ cup chopped green pepper
- 1 cup (4 ounces) shredded cheddar cheese, divided
- 2 tablespoons ketchup
  Salt and pepper to taste

1. Trim the ends off zucchini. Cut zucchini in half lengthwise; scoop out pulp, leaving ½-in. shells. Finely chop pulp.

2. In a skillet, cook the beef, zucchini pulp, onion, mushrooms and peppers over medium heat until meat is no longer pink; drain. Remove from the heat. Add ½ cup cheese, ketchup, salt and pepper; mix well. Spoon into the zucchini shells. Place in a greased 13-in. x 9-in. baking dish. Sprinkle remaining cheese over the top.

3. Bake, uncovered, at 350° for 25-30 minutes or until zucchini is tender.

Easy-to-Stuff Manicotti

PREP: 20 MIN. **BAKE:** 30 MIN. **MAKES:** 6-8 SERVINGS

- 1 package (8 ounces) manicotti shells
- 1 pound ground beef
- ½ cup chopped onion
- 1 jar (24 ounces) spaghetti sauce
- 14 pieces string cheese
- 1½ cups (6 ounces) shredded part-skim mozzarella cheese

1. Cook manicotti according to package directions. Meanwhile, in a large skillet, cook beef and onion over medium heat until meat is no longer pink; drain. Stir in spaghetti sauce. Spread half of the meat sauce into a greased 13-in. x 9-in. baking dish.

2. Drain manicotti; stuff each shell with a piece of string cheese. Place over meat sauce; top with remaining sauce. Cover and bake at 350° for 25-30 minutes or until heated through.

3. Sprinkle with mozzarella cheese. Bake 5-10 minutes longer or until the cheese is melted.

❝It's so easy to make my simplified version of manicotti. I fill each pasta shell with a piece of string cheese for a deliciously gooey center, then I top the shells with a beefy tomato sauce.❞

— **SUZANNE RUNTZ** MOUNT PLEASANT, SOUTH CAROLINA

Spiral Pepperoni Pizza Bake

PREP: 30 MIN. **BAKE:** 40 MIN.
MAKES: 12 SERVINGS

- 1 package (16 ounces) spiral pasta
- 2 pounds ground beef
- 1 large onion, chopped
- 1 teaspoon salt
- ½ teaspoon pepper
- 2 cans (15 ounces each) pizza sauce
- ½ teaspoon garlic salt
- ½ teaspoon Italian seasoning
- 2 eggs
- 2 cups milk
- ½ cup shredded Parmesan cheese
- 4 cups (16 ounces) shredded part-skim mozzarella cheese
- 1 package (3½ ounces) sliced pepperoni

1. Cook pasta according to package directions. Meanwhile, in a Dutch oven, cook the beef, onion, salt and pepper over medium heat until meat is no longer pink; drain. Stir in the pizza sauce, garlic salt and Italian seasoning; remove from the heat and set aside.

2. In a small bowl, combine the eggs, milk and Parmesan cheese. Drain pasta; toss with egg mixture. Transfer to a greased 3-qt. baking dish. Top with beef mixture, mozzarella cheese and pepperoni.

3. Cover and bake at 350° for 20 minutes. Uncover; bake 20-25 minutes longer or until golden brown and a thermometer reads 160°.

Oven-Baked Burgers

A crispy coating mix is the secret ingredient that dresses up these burgers you bake in the oven instead of grill or fry. I like to use a sweet and spicy steak sauce for the best flavor.

— **MIKE GOLDMAN** ARDEN HILLS, MINNESOTA

PREP/TOTAL TIME: 30 MIN.
MAKES: 4 SERVINGS

- ¼ cup steak sauce
- 2 tablespoons plus ⅓ cup seasoned coating mix, divided
- 1 pound ground beef
- 4 hamburger buns, split
- 4 lettuce leaves

1. In a bowl, combine the steak sauce and 2 tablespoons of coating mix. Crumble beef over mixture and mix well. Shape into four 3½-in. patties. Dip both sides of patties in remaining coating. Place on an ungreased baking sheet.

2. Bake at 350° for 20 minutes or until a thermometer reads 160° and juices run clear, turning once. Serve on buns with lettuce.

CASSEROLES & OVEN ENTREES

My grandmother used to fix this yummy dish for my Girl Scout troop when I was growing up. Now I make it for my stepdaughter's scout troop. It's easy to prepare, so I don't mind when the girls beg me to make it.

— **KIMBERLY HOWLAND** FREMONT, MICHIGAN

SPIRAL PEPPERONI PIZZA BAKE

Corn Bread Sloppy Joes

PREP/TOTAL TIME: 30 MIN.
MAKES: 6 SERVINGS

- 1 package (8½ ounces) corn bread/muffin mix
- 2 pounds ground beef
- ½ cup chopped onion
- 1 jar (24 ounces) spaghetti sauce
- 1 cup frozen corn
- 1 can (4 ounces) chopped green chilies, drained
- 2 envelopes sloppy joe mix
- 1 cup (4 ounces) shredded cheddar cheese

1. Prepare and bake corn bread according to package directions.
2. Meanwhile, in a large skillet, cook beef and onion over medium heat until meat is no longer pink; drain. Stir in the spaghetti sauce, corn, chilies and sloppy joe mix.
3. Bring to a boil. Reduce heat; simmer, uncovered, for 10 minutes.
4. Sprinkle with cheese; cover and cook for 1 minute or until cheese is melted.
5. Cut the corn bread into six pieces; cut each piece in half. Place on serving plates and top with sloppy joe mixture.

66If your grocery store's bakery offers ready-to-eat corn bread, you'll have a big jump on this easy and casual dinner.99

— **TASTE OF HOME TEST KITCHEN**

Italian Shepherd's Pies

Made in individual baking cups, these hearty little pies have biscuit-like tops and a saucy filling. You can also prepare the mixture in a 1½-quart casserole dish.

— **SONYA LABBE** WEST HOLLYWOOD, CALIFORNIA

PREP: 20 MIN. **BAKE:** 15 MIN. **MAKES:** 4 SERVINGS

- 1 pound ground beef
- 1 medium onion, finely chopped
- 2 cups marinara sauce
- ⅛ teaspoon salt
- ⅛ teaspoon pepper

TOPPING

- 1 cup all-purpose flour
- ¼ cup grated Parmesan cheese
- 1½ teaspoons baking powder
- ½ teaspoon salt
- ¼ teaspoon Italian seasoning
- ½ cup 2% milk
- ¼ cup butter, melted

1. In a large skillet, cook beef and onion over medium heat until meat is no longer pink; drain. Add the marinara sauce, salt and pepper; cook and stir for 8-10 minutes or until thickened. Spoon into four 8-oz. ramekins or custard cups; set aside.
2. In a small bowl, combine the flour, cheese, baking powder, salt and Italian seasoning. Stir in milk and butter just until moistened. Spoon dough over meat mixture.
3. Place ramekins on a baking sheet. Bake at 450° for 12-15 minutes or until tops are golden brown.

Spoon Bread Tamale Bake

Here's our favorite comfort food on chilly winter nights. My family loves the authentic tamale flavor, and I like that it's less work than tamales. Use 2 beaten eggs instead of egg substitute if you prefer.

— **MARJORIE MERSEREAU** CORVALLIS, OREGON

PREP: 25 MIN. **BAKE:** 30 MIN. **MAKES:** 8 SERVINGS

- 1½ **pounds lean ground beef (90% lean)**
- 1 **large onion, chopped**
- 1 **small green pepper, chopped**
- 1 **garlic clove, minced**
- 1 **can (28 ounces) diced tomatoes, undrained**
- 1½ **cups frozen corn**
- 1 **can (2¼ ounces) sliced ripe olives, drained**
- 4½ **teaspoons chili powder**
- ½ **teaspoon salt**
- ¼ **teaspoon pepper**
- ½ **cup cornmeal**
- 1 **cup water**

TOPPING
- 1½ **cups fat-free milk, divided**
- ½ **cup cornmeal**
- ½ **teaspoon salt**
- ½ **cup shredded reduced-fat cheddar cheese**
- 2 **tablespoons butter**
- ½ **cup egg substitute**

1. In a Dutch oven coated with cooking spray, cook the beef, onion, green pepper and garlic over medium heat until meat is no longer pink; drain. Stir in the tomatoes, corn, olives, chili powder, salt and pepper. Bring to a boil. Reduce heat; simmer, uncovered, for 5 minutes.

2. Combine cornmeal and water until smooth; gradually stir into the pan. Bring to a boil. Reduce heat; simmer, uncovered, for

10 minutes, stirring occasionally. Transfer to a 2½-qt. baking dish coated with cooking spray.

3. In a small saucepan, bring 1 cup milk to a boil. Combine the cornmeal, salt and remaining milk; slowly whisk into boiling milk. Cook and stir until mixture returns to a boil. Reduce heat; cook and stir for 3-4 minutes or until slightly thickened.

4. Remove from the heat; stir in cheese and butter until melted. Stir in egg substitute. Pour over meat mixture. Bake, uncovered, at 375° for 30-40 minutes or until topping is lightly browned.

Traditional Meat Loaf

Topped with a sweet sauce, this meat loaf tastes so good that you might want to double the recipe so everyone can have seconds. It also freezes well.

— **GAIL GRAHAM** MAPLE RIDGE, BRITISH COLUMBIA

PREP: 15 MIN. **BAKE:** 1 HOUR + STANDING **MAKES:** 6 SERVINGS

- 1 **egg, lightly beaten**
- ⅔ **cup 2% milk**
- 3 **slices bread, crumbled**
- 1 **cup (4 ounces) shredded cheddar cheese**
- 1 **medium onion, chopped**
- ½ **cup finely shredded carrot**
- 1 **teaspoon salt**
- ¼ **teaspoon pepper**
- 1½ **pounds ground beef**
- ¼ **cup packed brown sugar**
- ¼ **cup ketchup**
- 1 **tablespoon prepared mustard**

1. In a large bowl, combine the first eight ingredients. Crumble beef over mixture and mix well. Shape into a loaf. Place in a greased 9-in. x 5-in. loaf pan.

2. In a small bowl, combine the brown sugar, ketchup and mustard; spread over loaf. Bake at 350° for 60-75 minutes or until no pink remains and a thermometer reads 160°. Drain. Let stand for 10 minutes before slicing.

This delicious homemade pizza has a crispy, golden crust. Feel free to use whatever toppings your family enjoys.

— **MARIANNE EDWARDS** LAKE STEVENS, WASHINGTON

HOMEMADE PIZZA

Homemade Pizza

PREP: 25 MIN. + RISING
BAKE: 25 MIN.
MAKES: 2 PIZZAS (3 SERVINGS EACH)

- 1 package (¼ ounce) active dry yeast
- 1 teaspoon sugar
- 1¼ cups warm water (110° to 115°)
- ¼ cup canola oil
- 1 teaspoon salt
- 3½ cups all-purpose flour
- ½ pound ground beef
- 1 small onion, chopped
- 1 can (15 ounces) tomato sauce
- 3 teaspoons dried oregano
- 1 teaspoon dried basil
- 1 medium green pepper, diced
- 2 cups (8 ounces) shredded part-skim mozzarella cheese

1. In large bowl, dissolve yeast and sugar in water; let stand for 5 minutes. Add oil and salt. Stir in flour, a cup at a time, until a soft dough forms.
2. Turn onto floured surface; knead until smooth and elastic, about 2-3 minutes. Place in a greased bowl, turning once to grease the top. Cover and let rise in a warm place until doubled, about 45 minutes. Meanwhile, cook beef and onion over medium heat until no longer pink; drain.
3. Punch down dough; divide in half. Press each into a greased 12-in. pizza pan. Combine the tomato sauce, oregano and basil; spread over each crust. Top with beef mixture, green pepper and cheese.
4. Bake at 400° for 25-30 minutes or until crust is lightly browned.

 Baked items depend on correct oven temperature to rise and cook properly. For best results, first check that oven racks are properly positioned. Then preheat the oven while you prepare the recipe.

Stuffed Acorn Squash

Stuffed squash is an easy and elegant dish that can be served for special-occasion meals as well as everyday dinners. It's a must for our family when the garden squash is in bloom.

— **RUTH STONE** LINDSAY, NEBRASKA

PREP: 55 MIN. **BAKE:** 15 MIN. **MAKES:** 4 SERVINGS

- 2 large acorn squash, halved and seeded
- 1 cup water
- ¾ pound ground beef
- 1 celery rib, chopped
- 1 small onion, chopped
- 1 medium tart apple, chopped
- 1 cup cooked rice
- ¼ cup sunflower kernels
- 1 teaspoon curry powder
- 1 egg, beaten
- 5 teaspoons brown sugar, divided
- 1¼ teaspoons salt, divided
- 4 teaspoons butter

1. Invert squash in two ungreased 13-in. x 9-in. baking dishes. Add water and cover with foil. Bake at 375° for 40-45 minutes or until tender.

2. Meanwhile, cook the beef, celery and onion over medium heat until meat is no longer pink and vegetables are tender; drain. Add the apple, rice, sunflower kernels and curry. Cook and stir until apple is tender. Remove from the heat. Stir in the egg, 1 teaspoon brown sugar and ¾ teaspoon salt.

3. Place squash cut side up on a baking sheet. Place 1 teaspoon of the remaining brown sugar and 1 teaspoon of butter in each half. Sprinkle with remaining salt. Fill with meat mixture.

4. Bake, uncovered, at 375° for 15-20 minutes or until squash is heated through.

Meat Lover's Pizza Bake

PREP: 20 MIN. **BAKE:** 25 MIN. + STANDING **MAKES:** 6 SERVINGS

- 1 pound ground beef
- ½ cup chopped green pepper
- 1 can (15 ounces) pizza sauce
- 1 package (3½ ounces) sliced pepperoni, chopped
- 1 can (2¼ ounces) sliced ripe olives, drained
- 2 cups (8 ounces) shredded part-skim mozzarella cheese
- ¾ cup biscuit/baking mix
- 2 eggs
- ¾ cup milk

1. In a large skillet, cook beef and green pepper over medium heat until meat is no longer pink; drain. Stir in the pizza sauce, pepperoni and olives. Transfer to a greased 11-in. x 7-in. baking dish. Sprinkle with cheese.

2. In a small bowl, combine the biscuit mix, eggs and milk until blended. Pour evenly over cheese.

3. Bake, uncovered, at 400° for 25-30 minutes or until golden brown. Let stand for 10 minutes before serving.

❝Here's a yummy pizza casserole that's hearty with ground beef and pepperoni. Instead of a typical pizza crust, it has an easy topping made with biscuit mix.❞

— **CAROL OAKES** STURGIS, MICHIGAN

Mashed Potato Beef Casserole

My mother's old cookbook is the source for this warm and satisfying dish. The smudges and splatters show that Mom used the recipe often to feed our family. Now I prepare it for our children and grandchildren.

— **HELEN MCGEORGE** ABBOTSFORD, BRITISH COLUMBIA

PREP: 30 MIN. **BAKE:** 25 MIN. **MAKES:** 4-6 SERVINGS

- 2 **bacon strips, diced**
- 1 **pound ground beef**
- 1¾ **cups sliced fresh mushrooms**
- 1 **large onion, finely chopped**
- 1 **large carrot, finely chopped**
- 1 **celery rib, finely chopped**
- 3 **tablespoons all-purpose flour**
- 1 **cup beef broth**
- 1 **tablespoon Worcestershire sauce**
- 1 **teaspoon dried tarragon**
- ¼ **teaspoon pepper**
- 3 **cups hot mashed potatoes**
- ¾ **cup shredded cheddar cheese, divided**
  Paprika

1. In a large skillet, cook bacon until crisp; drain, reserving 1 teaspoon drippings. Set bacon aside. Cook beef in drippings over medium heat until no longer pink; drain.
2. Toss mushrooms, onion, carrot and celery in flour; add to skillet with the broth, Worcestershire sauce, tarragon and pepper. Bring to a boil. Reduce heat; simmer, uncovered, 15-20 minutes or until the vegetables are tender.
3. Add bacon; transfer to a greased 2-qt. baking dish. Combine potatoes and ½ cup of cheese; spread over beef mixture. Sprinkle with paprika and remaining cheese.
4. Bake, uncovered, at 350° for 20-25 minutes or until heated through. Broil 4 in. from the heat for 5 minutes or until bubbly.

Sun-Dried Tomato Meat Loaf

Meat loaf receives an Italian flair thanks to popular herbs and tangy sun-dried tomatoes. The recipe yields a large loaf, and extra slices make tasty sandwiches.

— **TASTE OF HOME TEST KITCHEN**

PREP: 25 MIN. **BAKE:** 55 MIN. + STANDING **MAKES:** 10 SERVINGS

- 1¼ **cups sun-dried tomatoes (not packed in oil)**
- 3 **cups boiling water**
- ½ **cup chopped onion**
- ½ **cup chopped green pepper**
- 2 **teaspoons canola oil**
- 1 **egg, lightly beaten**
- ½ **cup milk**
- 1 **cup soft bread crumbs**
- 2 **teaspoons dried basil**
- 1 **teaspoon dried oregano**
- 1 **teaspoon salt**
- 1 **teaspoon pepper**
- ½ **teaspoon dried thyme**
- 1½ **pounds ground beef**
- ¼ **cup ketchup**

1. In a large bowl, combine tomatoes and water; let stand for 15 minutes or until softened. Meanwhile, in a small skillet, saute onion and green pepper in oil until tender. In a large bowl, combine the egg, milk and bread crumbs.
2. Drain and chop the tomatoes; set aside ¼ cup for topping. Add onion mixture, basil, oregano, salt, pepper, thyme and remaining chopped tomatoes to the egg mixture. Crumble beef over mixture and mix well. Shape into a loaf in an ungreased 13-in. x 9-in. baking dish.
3. Combine ketchup and reserved tomatoes; spread over loaf. Bake, uncovered, at 350° for 55-60 minutes or until no pink remains and a thermometer reads 160°. Drain; let stand for 10 minutes before slicing.

Broccoli Beef Supper

PREP: 25 MIN. **BAKE:** 35 MIN.
MAKES: 4-6 SERVINGS

- ¾ cup uncooked long grain rice
- 1 pound ground beef
- 1½ cups fresh broccoli florets
- 1 can (10¾ ounces) condensed broccoli cheese soup, undiluted
- ½ cup milk
- 1 teaspoon salt-free seasoning blend
- 1 teaspoon salt
- ½ teaspoon pepper
- ½ cup dry bread crumbs
- 2 tablespoons butter, melted

1. Cook rice according to package directions. In a large skillet, cook beef over medium heat until no longer pink; drain. Stir in the rice, broccoli, soup, milk, seasoning blend, salt and pepper.

2. Transfer to a greased 2-qt. baking dish. Toss bread crumbs and butter; sprinkle over beef mixture.

3. Cover and bake at 350° for 30 minutes. Uncover; bake 5-10 minutes longer or until heated through.

Taco Meat Loaf

The kids will love this tasty meat loaf. I like to serve it with assorted taco toppings.

— **CATHY STREETER**
DE KALB JUNCTION, NEW YORK

PREP: 15 MIN. **BAKE:** 1½ HOURS
MAKES: 8 SERVINGS

- 1 cup crushed saltines (about 30 crackers)
- 1 envelope taco seasoning
- ½ cup ketchup
- 1 can (4 ounces) mushroom stems and pieces, drained
- 1 can (2¼ ounces) sliced ripe olives, drained
- 1 small onion, chopped
- 2 eggs, lightly beaten
- 2 tablespoons Worcestershire sauce
- 2 pounds lean ground beef (90% lean)
  Salsa, sour cream, shredded cheddar cheese and additional olives, optional

1. In a large bowl, combine the first eight ingredients. Crumble beef over mixture and mix well. Press into a greased 9-in. x 5-in. loaf pan.

2. Bake meat loaf, uncovered, at 350° for 1½ hours or until no pink remains and a thermometer reads 160°. Serve with salsa, sour cream, cheese and olives if desired.

When I put together a cookbook for our family reunion, my sister submitted this easy dinner. My husband and our boys really like when I make it.

— **NITA GRAFFIS** DOVE CREEK, COLORADO

BROCCOLI BEEF SUPPER

Spud-Stuffed Peppers

I created a yummy stuffed pepper recipe that uses fresh potatoes from my garden instead of the rice you'd usually see.

— **JOYCE JANDERA** HANOVER, KANSAS

PREP: 25 MIN. **BAKE:** 40 MIN.
MAKES: 2 SERVINGS

- 2 **medium green peppers**
- ½ **pound lean ground beef (90% lean)**
- 1 **medium potato, peeled and grated**
- 1½ **teaspoons chili powder**
- ¼ **teaspoon salt**
  Dash coarsely ground pepper
- ¼ **cup shredded reduced-fat cheddar cheese**

1. Cut tops off peppers and remove seeds. In a large saucepan, cook peppers in boiling water for 4-5 minutes. Drain and rinse in cold water; invert on paper towels.
2. In a nonstick skillet, cook beef and potato over medium heat until meat is no longer pink; drain. Stir in the chili powder, salt and pepper. Spoon into peppers.
3. Place in a small baking pan coated with cooking spray. Cover and bake at 350° for 35 minutes. Sprinkle with cheese. Bake, uncovered, 5-10 minutes longer or until cheese is melted.

top tip

When I make chowder, I like to add leftover scalloped potatoes or other cooked potato dishes to it. The soup that results is more flavorful and filling.

—**JEAN J.**
CHULA VISTA, CALIFORNIA

Winter Day Dinner

In the middle of winter, I often rely on this recipe to warm us up! My husband doesn't like noodles, so I have lots of different ways to serve potatoes.

— **LINDA HAGEDORN** ROCKVILLE, MARYLAND

PREP: 25 MIN. **BAKE:** 1½ HOURS **MAKES:** 8 SERVINGS

- 1½ **pounds ground beef**
- 1 **medium onion, chopped**
- 2 **tablespoons Worcestershire sauce**
- 1 **teaspoon salt**
- ½ **teaspoon pepper**
- 8 **medium potatoes, sliced**
- 1 **package (16 ounces) frozen peas, thawed**

CHEESE SAUCE
- ¼ **cup butter, cubed**
- ⅓ **cup all-purpose flour**
- ½ **teaspoon salt**
- ¼ **teaspoon pepper**
- 2 **cups milk**
- 4 **ounces process cheese (Velveeta), cubed**

1. In a large skillet, cook the beef and onion over medium heat until meat is no longer pink; drain. Stir in the Worcestershire sauce, salt and pepper.
2. Place half of the potatoes in a greased 13-in. x 9-in. baking dish; layer with meat mixture, peas and remaining potatoes. Set aside.
3. In a large saucepan, melt butter over medium heat. Stir in the flour, salt and pepper until smooth. Gradually stir in milk. Bring to a boil; cook and stir for 2 minutes or until thickened. Stir in cheese until melted. Pour over potatoes.
4. Cover and bake at 350° for 1½ hours or until potatoes are tender.

Overnight Mexican Manicotti

Serve this hearty entree with tortilla chips and homemade salsa for an easy plan-ahead meal when company's coming.

— LUCY SHIFTON WICHITA, KANSAS

PREP: 15 MIN. + CHILLING **BAKE:** 65 MIN. + STANDING **MAKES:** 8 SERVINGS

- 1 pound lean ground beef
- 1 can (16 ounces) refried beans
- 2½ teaspoons chili powder
- 1½ teaspoons dried oregano
- 1 package (8 ounces) uncooked manicotti shells
- 2½ cups water
- 1 jar (16 ounces) picante sauce
- 2 cups (16 ounces) sour cream
- 1 cup (4 ounces) shredded Monterey Jack or Mexican cheese blend
- ¼ cup sliced green onions
  Sliced ripe olives, optional

1. In a large bowl, combine the uncooked beef, beans, chili powder and oregano. Spoon into uncooked manicotti shells; arrange in a greased 13-in. x 9-in. baking dish. Combine water and picante sauce; pour over shells. Cover and refrigerate overnight.

2. Remove from the refrigerator 30 minutes before baking. Cover and bake at 350° for 1 hour. Uncover; spoon sour cream over the top. Sprinkle with cheese, onions and olives if desired. Bake 5-10 minutes longer or until the cheese is melted.

Finnish Beef Pie

We enjoy this traditional meat pie year-round, but my family especially appreciates it during hunting season. This beloved recipe is one I'll be sure to pass on to our seven children.

— LAUREL SKOOG FRAZEE, MINNESOTA

PREP: 25 MIN. + CHILLING
BAKE: 1¼ HOURS **MAKES:** 6-8 SERVINGS

- 1 cup water
- 1 teaspoon salt
- 1 cup shortening
- 3 cups all-purpose flour

FILLING

- 4 cups shredded peeled potatoes
- 1½ pounds lean ground beef
- 2 cups shredded carrots
- 1 medium onion, chopped
- ½ cup shredded peeled rutabaga
- 1½ teaspoons salt
- ¼ teaspoon pepper

1. In a large saucepan, combine water and salt; bring to a boil. Remove from the heat. Stir in the shortening until melted. Add the flour; stir until a soft ball forms.

2. Cover and refrigerate until dough is cooled, about 1 hour.

3. Divide dough in half. On a floured surface, roll one portion of dough to fit the bottom of a 13-in. x 9-in. baking dish. Line ungreased dish with pastry.

4. In a large bowl, combine filling ingredients. Spoon into crust. Roll out remaining pastry to fit top of dish.

5. Place over filling; press edges with a fork to seal. Cut slits in top. Bake at 350° for 1¼ hours or until golden brown.

Apple Meat Loaf

PREP: 15 MIN. **BAKE:** 40 MIN. **MAKES:** 3 SERVINGS

- 1 small onion, finely chopped
- 2 teaspoons butter
- ¾ cup shredded peeled apple
- ½ cup soft bread crumbs
- 1 egg
- 4 teaspoons ketchup
- 1 teaspoon Dijon mustard
- ½ teaspoon salt
- ¼ teaspoon pepper
  Dash ground allspice
- ¾ pound lean ground beef

1. In a small skillet, saute onion in butter until tender. In a large bowl, combine the apple, bread crumbs, egg, ketchup, mustard, salt, pepper and allspice. Stir in onion. Crumble beef over mixture and mix well. Shape into a 6-in. x 5-in. loaf.

2. Place in an 8-in. square baking dish coated with cooking spray. Bake, uncovered, at 350° for 40-45 minutes or until no pink remains and a thermometer reads 160°.

> ❝I put a little twist on the wonderful meat loaf my mom made when I was a kid. Apple gives it a hint of sweetness and helps keep it moist.❞
> — **DEB WILLIAMS** PEORIA, ARIZONA

Beef 'n' Eggplant Pie

Everyone likes eggplant when they taste it in a rich and savory pie. If the eggplant is large and the skin seems tough, it's a good idea to peel it first.

— **AUDREY NEMETH** CHESTERVILLE, MAINE

PREP: 20 MIN. **BAKE:** 20 MIN. + STANDING **MAKES:** 4-6 SERVINGS

- ¼ cup butter, cubed
- 2 cups cubed eggplant
- ¾ pound ground beef
- ½ cup finely chopped onion
- 1 celery rib with leaves, chopped
- 1 garlic clove, minced
- 1 can (8 ounces) tomato sauce
- 1 tablespoon minced fresh parsley
- 1 tablespoon dried oregano
- 1 teaspoon salt
- ⅛ teaspoon pepper
- 1 unbaked pastry shell (9 inches)
- ½ to 1 cup shredded part-skim mozzarella cheese

1. In a small skillet, melt butter. Add eggplant; saute until tender, about 5 minutes. In a large skillet, cook the beef, onion, celery and garlic over medium heat until meat is no longer pink; drain. Add the eggplant, tomato sauce, parsley, oregano, salt and pepper; bring to a boil. Remove from the heat.

2. Prick pastry shell with a fork. Add beef mixture. Bake at 375° for 20-25 minutes. Sprinkle with cheese. Bake 5-10 minutes longer or until cheese is melted. Let stand for 10 minutes before cutting pie.

Baked Ziti

I enjoy making ziti for family and friends. It's easy to prepare, and I like to get creative with the sauce. For example, I sometimes add my home-canned tomatoes, mushrooms or vegetables.

— ELAINE ANDERSON
NEW GALILEE, PENNSYLVANIA

PREP: 20 MIN. **BAKE:** 45 MIN. + STANDING
MAKES: 6-8 SERVINGS

12	ounces uncooked ziti or small tube pasta
2	pounds ground beef
1	jar (24 ounces) spaghetti sauce
2	eggs, beaten
1	carton (15 ounces) ricotta cheese
2½	cups (10 ounces) shredded mozzarella cheese, divided
½	cup grated Parmesan cheese

1. Cook pasta according to package directions. Meanwhile, in a large skillet, cook beef over medium heat until no longer pink; drain. Stir in spaghetti sauce.

2. In a large bowl, combine the eggs, ricotta cheese, 1½ cups mozzarella and the Parmesan cheese. Drain pasta; add to cheese mixture and stir until blended.

3. Spoon a third of the meat sauce into a greased 13-in. x 9-in. baking dish; top with half of the pasta mixture. Repeat layers. Top with remaining meat sauce.

4. Cover and bake at 350° for 40 minutes or until a thermometer reads 160°. Uncover; sprinkle with remaining mozzarella cheese. Bake 5-10 minutes longer or until cheese is melted. Let stand for 15 minutes before serving.

Nacho Potato Casserole

I created this recipe for my family because we all love Mexican-style food. It was an instant success with them and so easy to prepare for me.

— GLORIA WARCZAK CEDARBURG, WISCONSIN

PREP: 20 MIN. **BAKE:** 1¼ HOURS + STANDING **MAKES:** 8 SERVINGS

2	pounds lean ground beef (90% lean)
¾	cup chopped onion, divided
1	envelope taco seasoning
1	can (8 ounces) tomato sauce
¾	cup water
1	can (4 ounces) chopped green chilies, drained
1	can (16 ounces) kidney beans, rinsed and drained
1	package (24 ounces) frozen O'Brien potatoes, thawed
1	can (10¾ ounces) condensed nacho cheese soup, undiluted
½	cup milk
¼	cup chopped green pepper
1	teaspoon Worcestershire sauce
¼	teaspoon sugar
	Paprika

1. In a large skillet, cook beef and ½ cup onion over medium heat until meat is no longer pink; drain. Stir in the taco seasoning, tomato sauce and water. Bring to boil; reduce heat and simmer for 1 minute.

2. Spread into a greased 13-in. x 9-in. baking dish. Top with the green chilies, beans and potatoes. In a large bowl, combine the soup, milk, green pepper, Worcestershire sauce, sugar and remaining onion; pour over potatoes. Sprinkle with paprika.

3. Cover and bake at 350° for 1 hour. Uncover and bake for 15 minutes or until lightly browned. Let stand for 10 minutes before cutting.

I've been stuffing pasta shells with different fillings for years, but my family enjoys this version with taco-seasoned meat the most. The frozen shells are so convenient, because you can take out only the number you need for a single-serving lunch or family dinner. Just add zippy taco sauce and bake.

— **MARGE HODEL** ROANOKE, ILLINOIS

Taco-Filled Pasta Shells

PREP: 20 MIN. + CHILLING
BAKE: 45 MIN.
MAKES: 2 CASSEROLES (6 SERVINGS EACH)

- 2 **pounds ground beef**
- 2 **envelopes taco seasoning**
- 1½ **cups water**
- 1 **package (8 ounces) cream cheese, cubed**
- 24 **uncooked jumbo pasta shells**
- ¼ **cup butter, melted**

ADDITIONAL INGREDIENTS
(FOR EACH CASSEROLE)

- 1 **cup salsa**
- 1 **cup taco sauce**
- 1 **cup (4 ounces) shredded cheddar cheese**
- 1 **cup (4 ounces) shredded Monterey Jack cheese**
- 1½ **cups crushed tortilla chips**
- 1 **cup (8 ounces) sour cream**
- 3 **green onions, chopped**

1. In a Dutch oven, cook beef over medium heat until no longer pink; drain. Stir in taco seasoning and water. Bring to a boil. Reduce the heat; simmer, uncovered, for 5 minutes. Stir in the cream cheese until melted.

2. Transfer filling to a bowl; cool. Chill for 1 hour.

3. Cook pasta according to package directions; drain. Gently toss with butter. Fill each shell with about 3 tablespoons of meat mixture. Place 12 shells in a freezer container. Cover and freeze for up to 3 months.

4. To prepare remaining shells, spoon salsa into a greased 9-in. square baking dish. Top with stuffed shells; spoon taco sauce over the top.

5. Cover and bake at 350° for 30 minutes. Uncover; sprinkle with cheeses and chips. Bake 15 minutes longer or until shells are heated through. Serve with sour cream and onions.

To use frozen shells: *Thaw in the refrigerator for 24 hours (shells will be partially frozen). Spoon salsa into a greased 9-in. square baking dish; top with shells and taco sauce. Cover and bake at 350° for 40 minutes. Uncover; sprinkle with cheeses and chips. Proceed as directed.*

TACO-FILLED PASTA SHELLS

Mexican Casserole

PREP: 20 MIN. **BAKE:** 40 MIN.
MAKES: 6 SERVINGS

- 1½ pounds ground beef
- 1 envelope taco seasoning
- ¾ cup water
- 1 can (16 ounces) refried beans
- ½ cup salsa
- 6 flour tortillas (6 inches)
- 2 cups frozen corn, thawed
- 2 cups (8 ounces) shredded cheddar cheese
  Shredded lettuce, chopped tomatoes, sliced ripe olives and sour cream, optional

1. In a large skillet, cook beef over medium heat until no longer pink; drain. Stir in taco seasoning and water. Bring to a boil. Reduce heat; simmer, uncovered, for 5 minutes.

2. Meanwhile, in a microwave-safe bowl, combine beans and salsa. Cover and microwave until spreadable.

3. Place three tortillas in a greased round 2½-qt. baking dish. Layer with half of the beef, bean mixture, corn and cheese; repeat layers.

4. Bake, uncovered, at 350° for 40-45 minutes or until cheese is melted. Let stand for 5 minutes. Serve with lettuce, tomatoes, olives and sour cream if desired.

Easy Beef & Potatoes

I sometimes add chopped onion when browning the ground beef for my easy-to-prep main dish. Sometimes I double the recipe to take to potlucks.

—SHIRLEY GOERING NEW ULM, MINNESOTA

PREP: 15 MIN. **BAKE:** 1¼ HOURS
MAKES: 4-6 SERVINGS

- 4 medium potatoes, peeled and sliced
- 1 pound ground beef, cooked and drained
- 1 can (10-¾ ounces) condensed cream of chicken soup, undiluted
- 1 can (10-¾ ounces) condensed vegetable beef soup, undiluted
- ½ teaspoon salt

In a large bowl, combine all ingredients. Transfer to a greased 2-qt. baking dish. Cover and bake at 350° for 1¼ to 1½ hours or until potatoes are tender.

Trying to use what I had on hand one day, I came up with this recipe. Choose your favorite taco seasoning and salsa to make the casserole as spicy or as mild as you like.
— **DAVID MILLS** INDIANAPOLIS, INDIANA

MEXICAN CASSEROLE

Mini Reuben Loaf

If you're a fan of Reuben sandwiches, you'll enjoy this satisfying rolled loaf made with rye bread crumbs, sauerkraut, corned beef and Swiss cheese. Served with potato dumplings or mashed potatoes, it's a satisfying meal.

— **DENISE WAHL** HOMER GLEN, ILLINOIS

PREP: 20 MIN. **BAKE:** 30 MIN.
MAKES: 2 SERVINGS

- 1 egg, beaten
- 2 tablespoons chopped onion
- 2 tablespoons 2% milk
- ⅓ pound lean ground beef
- 1¼ cups soft rye bread crumbs
- 2 tablespoons Dijon mustard
- ½ cup sauerkraut, rinsed and well drained
- 8 slices deli corned beef (about 2 ounces), divided
- ¾ cup shredded Swiss cheese, divided

1. In a small bowl, combine the egg, onion and milk. Crumble beef over mixture and mix well. Add bread crumbs; mix gently. On a piece of heavy-duty foil, pat beef mixture into an 8-in. x 6-in. rectangle.
2. Spread mustard over loaf to within 1 in. of edges. Layer with sauerkraut, six slices of corned beef and ½ cup Swiss cheese. Roll up jelly-roll style, starting with a short side and peeling foil away while rolling. Seal seam and ends.
3. Place meat loaf seam side down in a shallow 1-qt. baking dish coated with cooking spray. Bake, uncovered, at 350° for 25 minutes. Top with remaining corned beef and cheese. Bake 5 minutes longer or until no pink remains and a thermometer reads 160°. Using two large spatulas, carefully transfer meat loaf to a serving platter.

Sweet Potato Enchilada Stack

PREP: 20 MIN. **BAKE:** 20 MIN. **MAKES:** 6 SERVINGS

- 1 large sweet potato, peeled and cut into ½-inch cubes
- 1 tablespoon water
- 1 pound ground beef
- 1 medium onion, chopped
- 1 can (15 ounces) black beans, rinsed and drained
- 1 can (10 ounces) enchilada sauce
- 2 teaspoons chili powder
- ½ teaspoon dried oregano
- ½ teaspoon ground cumin
- 3 flour tortillas (8 inches)
- 2 cups (8 ounces) shredded cheddar cheese

1. In a large microwave-safe bowl, combine sweet potato and water. Cover and microwave on high for 4-5 minutes or until potato is almost tender.
2. Meanwhile, in a large skillet, cook beef and onion over medium heat until meat is no longer pink; drain. Stir in the beans, enchilada sauce, chili powder, oregano, cumin and sweet potato; heat through.
3. Place a flour tortilla in a greased 9-in. deep-dish pie plate; layer with a third of the beef mixture and cheese. Repeat layers twice. Bake at 400° for 20-25 minutes or until bubbly.

Editor's Note: *This recipe was tested in a 1,100-watt microwave.*

❝Mexican flavors abound in an awesome enchilada stack jam-packed with black beans and sweet potato.❞
—TASTE OF HOME TEST KITCHEN

Grandma's Potpie

My husband and father-in-law are both picky eaters, but they do enjoy this savory meat pie with a flaky golden crust. The recipe is from my husband's grandmother.

— **ANNETTE WHEATLEY** SYRACUSE, NEW YORK

PREP: 30 MIN. **BAKE:** 45 MIN. **MAKES:** 6 SERVINGS

1½ pounds ground beef
 1 teaspoon onion powder
   Salt to taste
 1 cup cubed peeled potatoes
 1 cup frozen mixed vegetables, thawed
 ¼ cup butter, cubed
 ¼ cup all-purpose flour
 1 can (14½ ounces) beef broth

CRUST
 2 cups all-purpose flour
 1 tablespoon baking powder
 1 teaspoon salt
 ¼ cup shortening
 ¾ cup milk
 1 tablespoon butter, melted

1. In a large skillet, cook beef over medium heat until no longer pink; drain. Stir in onion powder and salt. Transfer to a greased 9-in. square baking dish. Top with potatoes and vegetables.

2. Meanwhile, in a small skillet, melt the butter. Stir in flour until smooth; gradually add broth. Bring to a boil. Cook and stir for 2 minutes or until thickened. Pour over vegetables.

3. For crust, in a small bowl, combine the flour, baking powder and salt in a bowl. Cut in shortening until mixture resembles coarse crumbs. Stir in milk until a soft dough forms.

4. On a floured surface, roll dough into a 9-in. square. Place over filling; flute edges and cut slits in top. Brush with melted butter. Bake at 350° for 45 minutes or until golden brown.

Mexicali Meat Loaf

A cheesy Mexicorn topping gives this just-for-two meat loaf a Southwestern flair. I've made it for years because it's one of my husband's favorite meals.

— **LAURA WEBB** LINDSTROM, MINNESOTA

PREP: 20 MIN. **BAKE:** 40 MIN. **MAKES:** 2 SERVINGS

 2 tablespoons beaten egg
 2 tablespoons tomato juice
 ¼ cup quick-cooking oats
 ¾ teaspoon dried minced onion
 ¼ teaspoon salt
 ¼ teaspoon chili powder
 ⅛ teaspoon pepper
 ½ pound lean ground beef

TOPPING
 1½ teaspoons butter
 1½ teaspoons all-purpose flour
 ⅛ teaspoon salt
 ¼ cup 2% milk
 ¼ cup canned Mexicorn, drained
 2 slices process American cheese, diced
 2 green pepper rings, cut into strips

1. In a small bowl, combine the egg, tomato juice, oats, onion, salt, chili powder and pepper. Crumble beef over mixture and mix well. Pat into an ungreased 5¾-in. x 3-in. x 2-in. loaf pan. Bake, uncovered, at 350° for 20 minutes.

2. Meanwhile, in a small saucepan, melt butter. Stir in flour and salt until smooth; gradually add milk. Bring to a boil; cook and stir for 1 minute or until thickened. Remove from the heat. Stir in corn and cheese until cheese is melted.

3. Pour over meat loaf; top with green pepper strips. Bake 20-25 minutes longer or until meat is no longer pink and a thermometer reads 160°.

Creamy Beef with Biscuits

With 11 children, my mom had lots of cooking experience. She passed down her cooking knowledge and recipes to me. This home-style dinner was one that Mom usually served to company.

— **MARY MILLER** SHREVE, OHIO

PREP: 15 MIN. **BAKE:** 35 MIN. **MAKES:** 8-10 SERVINGS

- 2 **pounds ground beef**
- 1 **medium onion, chopped**
- 1 **package (8 ounces) cream cheese, cubed**
- 1 **can (10¾ ounces) condensed cream of mushroom soup, undiluted**
- ¾ **cup 2% milk**
- ½ **cup ketchup**
- ½ **teaspoon salt**
- ¼ **teaspoon pepper**
- 1 **tube (12 ounces) refrigerated buttermilk biscuits**

1. In a large skillet, cook beef and onion over medium heat until meat is no longer pink; drain. Add cream cheese, stirring until melted. Stir in the soup, milk, ketchup, salt and pepper.

2. Transfer to a greased 13-in. x 9-in. baking dish. Cover and bake at 375° for 15 minutes. Uncover; arrange biscuits over top. Bake 20-25 minutes longer or until biscuits are golden brown.

Mushroom-Stuffed Meat Loaf

I first tried this meat loaf after seeing it demonstrated on a local TV cooking program. Since then, I've served it time and again to family and guests. The flavorful stuffing sets it apart.

— **SHIRLEY LEISTER** WEST CHESTER, PENNSYLVANIA

PREP: 25 MIN. **BAKE:** 1 HOUR **MAKES:** 6 SERVINGS

- 2 **eggs**
- 2 **tablespoons milk**
- ¼ **cup ketchup**
- 1½ **teaspoons salt**
- ⅛ **teaspoon pepper**
- 1½ **pounds lean ground beef**
- **STUFFING**
- ½ **pound fresh mushrooms, sliced**
- 1 **medium onion, chopped**
- 2 **tablespoons butter**
- 2 **cups soft bread crumbs**
- 2 **tablespoons minced fresh parsley**
- ½ **teaspoon dried thyme**
- ½ **teaspoon salt**
- ⅛ **teaspoon pepper**

1. In a large bowl, beat eggs, milk, ketchup, salt and pepper. Add beef and mix well. Pat half of the meat mixture into a greased 9-in. x 5-in. loaf pan; set aside.

2. For stuffing, saute the mushrooms and onion in butter until tender, about 3 minutes. Add bread crumbs, parsley, thyme, salt and pepper; saute until crumbs are lightly browned.

3. Spoon over meat layer; cover with remaining meat mixture and press down gently. Bake at 350° for 1 hour or until a thermometer reads 160°, draining fat as necessary.

Chili Tots

Cook once and eat twice with this hearty Southwestern casserole. With help from a few convenience products, it quickly goes together before you freeze it or pop it into the oven to bake.

— **LINDA BALDWIN** LONG BEACH, CALIFORNIA

PREP: 15 MIN. **BAKE:** 35 MIN.
MAKES: 2 CASSEROLES (6 SERVINGS EACH)

- 1 **pound ground beef**
- 2 **cans (15 ounces each) chili without beans**
- 1 **can (8 ounces) tomato sauce**
- 1 **can (2¼ ounces) sliced ripe olives, drained**
- 1 **can (4 ounces) chopped green chilies**
- 2 **cups (8 ounces) shredded cheddar cheese**
- 1 **package (32 ounces) frozen Tater Tots**

1. In a large skillet, cook the beef over medium heat until no longer pink; drain. Stir in the chili, tomato sauce, olives and green chilies. Transfer to two greased 8-in. square baking dishes. Sprinkle with cheese; top with Tater Tots. Cover and freeze one casserole for up to 3 months.

2. Cover and bake the remaining casserole at 350° for 35-40 minutes or until heated through.

To use frozen casserole: *Remove from the freezer 30 minutes before baking (do not thaw). Cover and bake at 350° for 1¼ to 1½ hours or until heated through.*

4. Combine pizza sauce and 2 teaspoons Italian seasoning; spread half over crust. Sprinkle with beef mixture and mushrooms; cover with remaining pizza sauce mixture. Sprinkle with shredded cheeses and remaining Italian seasoning. Bake for 18-20 minutes or until cheese is melted and crust is golden brown.

Busy-Day Meat Loaf

Here's a tender meat loaf that's delicious for any day. It's great that you get two loaves from the recipe: one to enjoy today, and another to pull from the freezer on a busy night.

— **SHIRLEY SNYDER** PAYSON, ARIZONA

PREP: 15 MIN. **BAKE:** 55 MIN.
MAKES: 2 LOAVES (4-6 SERVINGS EACH)

    1 egg, lightly beaten
    1 cup beef broth
   ½ cup quick-cooking oats
    1 tablespoon dried minced onion
    2 teaspoons dried parsley flakes
    1 teaspoon salt
   ½ teaspoon pepper
  1½ pounds lean ground beef (90% lean)
    1 pound bulk pork sausage
    1 can (8 ounces) tomato sauce

1. In a large bowl, combine the first seven ingredients. Crumble beef and sausage over mixture and mix well. Pat into two greased 8-in. x 4-in. loaf pans. Top with tomato sauce.
2. Cover and freeze one meat loaf for up to 3 months. Bake the remaining loaf, uncovered, at 350° for 55-60 minutes until no pink remains and a thermometer reads 160°.

To use frozen meat loaf: *Thaw in the refrigerator overnight. Bake as directed.*

Stuffed-Crust Pizza

String cheese is the succulent surprise in the edges of this pizza's no-fail homemade crust. The hearty toppings can be varied to suit your preference.

— **RENAE JACOBSON** ELM CREEK, NEBRASKA

PREP: 40 MIN. **BAKE:** 20 MIN. **MAKES:** 8 SLICES

    1 pound ground beef
    1 small onion, chopped
  2½ to 3 cups all-purpose flour
    2 tablespoons Italian seasoning, divided
    1 package (¼ ounce) quick-rise yeast
    1 tablespoon sugar
   ½ teaspoon salt
    1 cup water
    3 tablespoons olive oil
    3 tablespoons cornmeal
    4 ounces string cheese
    1 can (15 ounces) pizza sauce
   ½ cup sliced fresh mushrooms
    1 cup (4 ounces) shredded part-skim mozzarella cheese
   ¼ cup shredded cheddar cheese

1. In a skillet, cook beef and onion over medium heat until meat is no longer pink; drain and set aside. In a bowl, combine 2½ cups flour, 1 tablespoon Italian seasoning, yeast, sugar and salt.
2. In a saucepan, heat water and oil to 120°-130°. Add to the dry ingredients; beat just until moistened. Stir in enough remaining flour to form a soft dough. Let rest for 5 minutes. Sprinkle cornmeal over a greased 14-in. pizza pan.
3. On a lightly floured surface, roll dough into a 15-in. circle. Transfer to prepared pan, letting dough drape over the edge. Cut string cheese in half lengthwise; place around edge of pan. Fold dough over string cheese; pinch to seal. Prick dough thoroughly with a fork. Bake at 375° for 5 minutes.

Crispy chow mein noodles top this twist on chop suey that's sure to be a family favorite.

— **WILLIE DEWAARD** CORALVILLE, IOWA

CHINESE BEEF CASSEROLE

Chinese Beef Casserole

PREP: 15 MIN. **BAKE:** 45 MIN.
MAKES: 8 SERVINGS

- 2 **pounds ground beef**
- 1 **cup chopped onion**
- 1 **cup chopped celery**
- 2 **cans (10¾ ounces each) condensed cream of mushroom soup, undiluted**
- 1 **can (14 ounces) bean sprouts, undrained**
- ¼ **cup reduced-sodium soy sauce**
- ½ **teaspoon pepper**
- 1 **cup uncooked long grain rice**
- 1 **can (8 ounces) sliced water chestnuts, drained**
- 2 **cups frozen peas, thawed**
- 1 **can (5 ounces) chow mein noodles**

1. In a large skillet, cook the beef, onion and celery over medium heat until meat is no longer pink; drain. Stir in the soup, bean sprouts, soy sauce and pepper. Bring to a boil. Pour into a greased 3-qt. baking dish. Stir in rice and water chestnuts.
2. Cover and bake at 350° for 30 minutes. Uncover; stir in peas and sprinkle with noodles. Bake 15-20 minutes longer or until heated through.

Salisbury Steak with Gravy

Here's a lightened-up twist on classic comfort food. The recipe was shared at a weight management meeting I attended, and my whole family really enjoys it. I like that it's so tasty and quick to prepare.

— **DANELLE WEIHER** VERNDALE, MINNESOTA

PREP: 15 MIN. **BAKE:** 50 MIN.
MAKES: 4 SERVINGS

- ½ **cup fat-free milk**
- 14 **fat-free saltines, crushed**
- 2 **tablespoons dried minced onion**
- 2 **teaspoons dried parsley flakes**
- 1 **pound lean ground beef (90% lean)**
- 1 **jar (12 ounces) fat-free beef gravy**
- 2 **tablespoons ketchup**
- 2 **teaspoons Worcestershire sauce**
- ¼ **teaspoon pepper**

1. In a large bowl, combine the milk, saltines, onion and parsley. Crumble beef over mixture and mix well. Shape into four patties. Place in an 8-in. square baking dish coated with cooking spray.
2. In a small bowl, combine the gravy, ketchup, Worcestershire and pepper; pour over patties. Bake, uncovered, at 350° for 50-55 minutes or until a thermometer reads 160°.

Black Bean Tamale Pie

PREP: 20 MIN. **BAKE:** 25 MIN.
MAKES: 6-8 SERVINGS

- ½ **pound ground beef**
- ½ **cup chopped onion**
- ½ **cup chopped green pepper**
- 1 **can (15 ounces) black beans, rinsed and drained**
- 1 **cup salsa**
- 1 **package (8½ ounces) corn bread/ muffin mix**
- ¼ **cup milk**
- 1 **egg**
- 2 **cups (8 ounces) shredded cheddar cheese, divided**
  Sour cream and sliced ripe olives, optional

1. In a large skillet, cook the beef, onion and green pepper over medium heat until meat is no longer pink; drain. Stir in beans and salsa; set aside.

2. In a large bowl, combine the muffin mix, milk, egg and 1 cup cheese. Pour into a greased 9-in. pie plate. Bake at 375° for 6 minutes.

3. Spoon beef mixture over crust, leaving a ½-in. edge. Bake for 15-18 minutes or until crust is golden brown. Sprinkle with remaining cheese. Bake 1-2 minutes longer or until cheese is melted. Serve with sour cream and olives if desired.

❝A corn bread mix makes an irresistible tamale crust in this pie loaded with beef and beans. For a change of pace, try topping it with lettuce, guacamole or extra salsa.❞

— **LAURA MORRIS** ST. JOSEPH, MISSOURI

CASSEROLES & OVEN ENTREES

BLACK BEAN TAMALE PIE

“What could be easier than an Italian-inspired meat loaf made in the slow cooker? No fuss, easy cleanup and great homemade flavor; it’s all right here!”

— **SHARON DELANEY-CHRONIS** SOUTH MILWAUKEE, WISCONSIN
about her recipe, Healthy Slow-Cooked Meat Loaf, on page 96

97

90

98

Slow Cooker

Chunky Pasta Sauce

PREP: 25 MIN. **COOK:** 6 HOURS
MAKES: 8 SERVINGS

- 1 **pound ground beef**
- ½ **pound ground pork**
- 2 **cans (28 ounces each) diced tomatoes, undrained**
- ½ **to 1 cup water**
- 1 **can (6 ounces) tomato paste**
- 1 **cup chopped carrots**
- 1 **medium onion, cut into wedges**
- 1 **medium sweet red pepper, cut into 1-inch pieces**
- 2 **tablespoons sugar**
- 2 **teaspoons minced garlic**
- 1 **teaspoon salt**
- 1 **teaspoon dried basil**
- 1 **teaspoon dried oregano**
- 1 **teaspoon pepper**
  Hot cooked bow tie pasta

1. In a large skillet, cook beef and pork over medium heat until meat is no longer pink; drain.

2. Transfer to a 3-qt. slow cooker. Stir in the tomatoes, water, tomato paste, vegetables, sugar, garlic and seasonings. Cover and cook on low for 6-8 hours or until vegetables are tender. Serve sauce over pasta.

Nacho Salsa Dip

This zesty dip is terrific for any get-together, and allows me to spend more time with my guests. I always have requests to bring it when my husband and I attend parties.

— **SALLY HULL** HOMESTEAD, FLORIDA

PREP: 15 MIN. **COOK:** 3 HOURS
MAKES: 7 CUPS

- 1 **pound ground beef**
- ⅓ **cup chopped onion**
- 2 **pounds process cheese (Velveeta), cubed**
- 1 **jar (16 ounces) chunky salsa**
- ¼ **teaspoon garlic powder**
  Tortilla chips or cubed French bread

1. In a large skillet, cook beef and onion over medium heat until meat is no longer pink; drain well.

2. Transfer to a greased 3-qt. slow cooker; stir in the cheese, salsa and garlic powder. Cover and cook on low for 3-4 hours or until heated through. Stir; serve warm with tortilla chips or cubed bread.

Your kitchen will smell heavenly when it's time to dish up this hearty meal. The sauce is loaded with beef, pork and lots of veggies. Add the extra 1/2 cup of water if you like your sauce a bit thinner.

— **CHRISTY HINRICHS** PARKVILLE, MISSOURI

CHUNKY PASTA SAUCE

Pineapple Baked Beans

Tangy pineapple dresses up these hearty baked beans. Brown the beef while you open cans and chop the vegetables, and it won't take long to get the side dish ready for the slow cooker.

— **GLADYS DE BOER** CASTLEFORD, IDAHO

PREP: 10 MIN. **COOK:** 6 HOURS
MAKES: 8 SERVINGS

- 1 **pound ground beef**
- 1 **can (28 ounces) baked beans**
- ¾ **cup pineapple tidbits, drained**
- 1 **jar (4½ ounces) sliced mushrooms, drained**
- 1 **large onion, chopped**
- 1 **large green pepper, chopped**
- ½ **cup barbecue sauce**
- 2 **tablespoons reduced-sodium soy sauce**
- 1 **garlic clove, minced**
- ½ **teaspoon salt**
- ¼ **teaspoon pepper**

1. In a large skillet, cook beef over medium heat until no longer pink; drain. Transfer to a 5-qt. slow cooker. Add the remaining ingredients and mix well.

2. Cover and cook on low for 6-8 hours or until bubbly.

Hobo Stew

I got the recipe for this easy stew from my husband's family in Missouri. I've yet to meet anyone who doesn't rave about it.

— **DICK BRAZEAL** CARLIN, NEVADA

PREP: 15 MIN. **COOK:** 6 HOURS
MAKES: 8 SERVINGS

- 1½ **pounds ground beef**
- 1 **medium onion, diced**
- 3 **cans (10¾ ounces each) condensed minestrone soup, undiluted**
- 2 **cans (15 ounces each) Ranch Style beans (pinto beans in seasoned tomato sauce)**
- 1 **can (10 ounces) diced tomatoes and green chilies, undrained**

1. In a large skillet, cook beef and onion over medium heat until meat is no longer pink; drain. Transfer to a 3-qt. slow cooker. Add the remaining ingredients and mix well.

2. Cover and cook on low for 6 hours or until heated through.

Slow-Cooked Lasagna

PREP: 45 MIN. **COOK:** 4¼ HOURS + STANDING **MAKES:** 6 SERVINGS

- 1 **pound ground beef**
- 1 **medium green pepper, chopped**
- 1 **medium onion, chopped**
- 1 **jar (26 ounces) herb and garlic pasta sauce**
- 4 **cups (16 ounces) shredded part-skim mozzarella cheese**
- 1 **carton (15 ounces) ricotta cheese**
- 1 **tablespoon Italian seasoning**
- ½ **teaspoon garlic powder**
- ½ **teaspoon salt**
- ¼ **teaspoon pepper**
- 4 **no-cook lasagna noodles**
- 2 **tablespoons shredded Parmesan cheese**

1. In a large skillet, cook the beef, green pepper and onion over medium heat until meat is no longer pink; drain. Stir in pasta sauce; heat through. In a large bowl, combine the mozzarella and ricotta cheeses, Italian seasoning, garlic powder, salt and pepper.

2. Spread 1 cup meat sauce in an oval 3-qt. slow cooker. Break one lasagna noodle into three pieces. Layer 1⅓ noodles over sauce, breaking noodles to fit as necessary. Top with ⅔ cup meat sauce and 1⅓ cups of cheese mixture. Repeat layers twice. Top with remaining sauce.

3. Cover and cook on low for 4-5 hours or until noodles are tender. Sprinkle with Parmesan cheese. Cover and cook 15 minutes longer. Let stand for 10 minutes before cutting.

"A traditional favorite is made super easy in the slow cooker. The finished dish even cuts well to make nice individual servings. You may need to break the noodles so they fit into the slow cooker crock.

— **REBECCA O'BRYAN** ALVATON, KENTUCKY

Cabbage Patch Stew

I like to serve steaming helpings of this hearty stew with thick, crusty slices of homemade bread. For a quicker prep, substitute coleslaw mix for the chopped cabbage.

— **KAREN ANN BLAND** GOVE, KANSAS

PREP: 20 MIN. **COOK:** 6 HOURS **MAKES:** 8 SERVINGS (2 QUARTS)

- 1 pound lean ground beef (90% lean)
- 1 cup chopped onion
- 2 celery ribs, chopped
- 11 cups coarsely chopped cabbage (about 2 pounds)
- 2 cans (14½ ounces each) stewed tomatoes, undrained
- 1 can (15 ounces) pinto beans, rinsed and drained
- 1 can (10 ounces) diced tomatoes with green chilies, undrained
- ½ cup ketchup
- 1 to 1½ teaspoons chili powder
- ½ teaspoon dried oregano
- ½ teaspoon pepper
- ¼ teaspoon salt
  Optional toppings: Shredded cheddar cheese and sour cream

1. In a large skillet, cook the beef, onion and celery over medium heat until meat is no longer pink; drain.

2. Transfer to a 5-qt. slow cooker. Stir in the cabbage, stewed tomatoes, beans, diced tomatoes, ketchup, chili powder, oregano, pepper and salt. Cover and cook on low for 6-8 hours or until cabbage is tender.

3. Serve with cheese and sour cream if desired.

Chili Coney Dogs

PREP: 20 MIN. **COOK:** 4 HOURS **MAKES:** 8 SERVINGS

- 1 pound lean ground beef (90% lean)
- 1 can (15 ounces) tomato sauce
- ½ cup water
- 2 tablespoons Worcestershire sauce
- 1 tablespoon dried minced onion
- ½ teaspoon garlic powder
- ½ teaspoon ground mustard
- ½ teaspoon chili powder
- ½ teaspoon pepper
  Dash cayenne pepper
- 8 hot dogs
- 8 hot dog buns, split
  Shredded cheddar cheese, relish and chopped onion, optional

1. In a large skillet, cook beef over medium heat until no longer pink; drain. Stir in the tomato sauce, water, Worcestershire sauce, onion and spices.

2. Place hot dogs in a 3-qt. slow cooker; top with beef mixture. Cover and cook on low for 4-5 hours or until heated through. Serve on buns with cheese, relish and onion if desired.

> "Everyone in our family, from smallest kids to oldest adults, adores these dogs. They're so easy to throw together and heat in the slow cooker."
>
> — **MICHELE HARRIS** VICKSBURG, MICHIGAN

Cincinnati Chili

The chocolate in this recipe threw me off at first, but now it's the only way I make chili. You'll find layers of flavor in a heartwarming, stick-to-your-ribs dish. It's well worth the time it takes.

— **JOYCE ALM** THORP, WASHINGTON

PREP: 25 MIN. **COOK:** 5½ HOURS **MAKES:** 10 SERVINGS

- 3 pounds ground beef
- 1½ cups chopped onions
- 1½ teaspoons minced garlic
- 2 cans (16 ounces each) kidney beans, rinsed and drained
- 2 cans (15 ounces each) tomato sauce
- 2 cups beef broth
- ¼ cup chili powder
- ¼ cup red wine vinegar
- ¼ cup Worcestershire sauce
- 1 ounce unsweetened chocolate, coarsely chopped
- 1½ teaspoons ground cinnamon
- 1½ teaspoons ground cumin
- 1 teaspoon salt
- 1 teaspoon dried oregano
- ½ teaspoon pepper
- ⅛ teaspoon ground cloves
  Hot cooked spaghetti
  Shredded cheddar cheese and sliced green onions, optional

1. In a Dutch oven, cook beef and onions over medium heat until meat is no longer pink. Add garlic; cook 1 minute longer. Drain.

2. In a 5-qt. slow cooker, combine the beans, tomato sauce, broth, chili powder, vinegar, Worcestershire sauce, chocolate and seasonings. Stir in beef mixture. Cover and cook on low for 5-6 hours or until heated through.

3. Serve with spaghetti. Garnish with cheese and green onions if desired.

Cowboy Calico Beans

This filling dish is a tradition at the table when my girlfriends and I go up North for a girls' weekend. The husbands and kids are left at home, but the slow cooker comes with us!

— **JULIE BUTSCH** HARTLAND, WISCONSIN

PREP: 30 MIN. **COOK:** 4 HOURS **MAKES:** 8 SERVINGS

- 1 pound lean ground beef (90% lean)
- 1 large sweet onion, chopped
- ½ cup packed brown sugar
- ¼ cup ketchup
- 3 tablespoons cider vinegar
- 2 tablespoons yellow mustard
- 1 can (16 ounces) butter beans, drained
- 1 can (16 ounces) kidney beans, rinsed and drained
- 1 can (15 ounces) pork and beans
- 1 can (15¼ ounces) lima beans, rinsed and drained

1. In a large skillet, cook beef and onion over medium heat until meat is no longer pink; drain.

2. Transfer to a 3-qt. slow cooker. Combine the brown sugar, ketchup, vinegar and mustard; add to meat mixture. Stir in the beans. Cover and cook on low for 4-5 hours or until mixture is heated through.

 top tip For an easy picnic salad, I cut leftover cooked spaghetti into small pieces, then mix it with mayonnaise, pickle juice, dill and whatever other potato salad ingredients I have on hand.
—**DOROTHY S.** NEW CASTLE, PENNSYLVANIA

Taco Chili

PREP: 30 MIN. **COOK:** 6 HOURS
MAKES: 11 SERVINGS (2¾ QUARTS)

- 2 pounds ground beef
- 1 can (16 ounces) kidney beans
- 1 can (15 ounces) pinto beans
- 1 can (15 ounces) black beans
- 1 can (14 ounces) hominy
- 1 can (10 ounces) diced tomatoes and green chilies, undrained
- 1 can (8 ounces) tomato sauce
- 1 small onion, chopped
- 1 envelope ranch salad dressing mix
- 1 envelope taco seasoning
- ½ teaspoon pepper
- 2 cans (14½ ounces each) diced tomatoes, undrained
- 1 can (4 ounces) chopped green chilies
  Corn chips, sour cream and shredded cheddar cheese, optional

1. In a large skillet, cook beef until no longer pink; drain. Transfer to a 5-qt. slow cooker. Rinse and drain beans and hominy; add to slow cooker. Stir in the tomatoes, tomato sauce, onion, salad dressing mix, taco seasoning and pepper.
2. In a blender, combine diced tomatoes and green chilies; cover and process until smooth. Add to the slow cooker. Cover and cook on low for 6-8 hours. Serve with corn chips, sour cream and cheese if desired.

Zippy Spanish Rice Soup

I created this recipe after ruining a dinner of Spanish rice. I salvaged the dish by adding green chiles, cilantro and more water.
— **MARILYN SCHETZ** CUYAHOGA FALLS, OHIO

PREP: 25 MIN **COOK:** 4 HOURS
MAKES: 8 SERVINGS (2 QUARTS)

- 1 pound lean ground beef (90% lean)
- 1 medium onion, chopped
- 3 cups water
- 1 jar (16 ounces) salsa
- 1 can (14½ ounces) diced tomatoes, undrained
- 1 jar (7 ounces) roasted sweet red peppers, drained and chopped
- 1 can (4 ounces) chopped green chilies
- 1 envelope taco seasoning
- 1 tablespoon dried cilantro flakes
- ½ cup uncooked converted rice

1. In a large skillet, cook beef and onion until meat is no longer pink; drain.
2. Transfer to a 4- or 5-qt. slow cooker. Stir in the remaining ingredients. Cover and cook on low for 4-5 hours or until rice is tender.

> Ranch dressing and taco seasoning infuse extra-special flavor into my hearty chili. Folks can't resist coming back for seconds!
> — **JULIE NEUHALFEN** GLENWOOD, IOWA

TACO CHILI

Hearty Cheese Tortellini

PREP: 30 MIN. **COOK:** 6¼ HOURS
MAKES: 6 SERVINGS

- ½ **pound bulk Italian sausage**
- ½ **pound lean ground beef (90% lean)**
- 1 **jar (24 ounces) marinara sauce**
- 1 **can (14½ ounces) Italian diced tomatoes**
- 1 **cup sliced fresh mushrooms**
- 1 **package (9 ounces) refrigerated cheese tortellini**
- 1 **cup (4 ounces) shredded part-skim mozzarella cheese**

1. In a small skillet, cook sausage and beef over medium heat until no longer pink; drain. Transfer to a 3-qt. slow cooker. Stir in the marinara sauce, tomatoes and mushrooms. Cover and cook on low for 6-7 hours or until heated through.

2. Prepare tortellini according to package directions; stir into meat mixture. Sprinkle with cheese. Cover and cook for 15 minutes or until cheese is melted.

"Simple enough for an everyday meal but good enough for company, this wonderful recipe is a favorite in our home. I serve it with steamed broccoli and fresh bread."

— CHRISTINE EILERTS TULSA, OKLAHOMA

Easy-Does-It Spaghetti

Combine ground beef, pasta, mushrooms and a handful of other ingredients in your slow cooker for a savory dish that will appeal to all ages. If you'd like, substitute ½ cup chopped onion for the dried minced onion.

— GENEVIEVE HRABE PLAINVILLE, KANSAS

PREP: 20 MIN. **COOK:** 5 HOURS **MAKES:** 6-8 SERVINGS

- 2 **pounds ground beef, cooked and drained**
- 1 **can (46 ounces) tomato juice**
- 1 **can (15 ounces) tomato sauce**
- 1 **can (8 ounces) mushroom stems and pieces, drained**
- 2 **tablespoons dried minced onion**
- 2 **teaspoon salt**
- 1 **teaspoon garlic powder**
- 1 **teaspoon ground mustard**
- ½ **teaspoon each ground allspice, mace and pepper**
- 1 **package (7 ounces) spaghetti, broken in half**

1. In a 5-qt. slow cooker, combine the beef, tomato juice, tomato sauce, mushrooms and seasonings. Cover and cook on high for 4-5 hours.

2. Stir in spaghetti. Cover and cook 1 hour longer or until spaghetti is tender.

Healthy Slow-Cooked Meat Loaf

PREP: 15 MIN. **COOK:** 3 HOURS **MAKES:** 8 SERVINGS

- 1 cup soft bread crumbs
- 1½ cups spaghetti sauce, divided
- 1 egg, lightly beaten
- 2 tablespoons dried minced onion
- 1 teaspoon salt
- ½ teaspoon garlic powder
- ½ teaspoon Italian seasoning
- ¼ teaspoon pepper
- 2 pounds lean ground beef (90% lean)

1. Cut four 20-in. x 3-in. strips of heavy-duty foil; crisscross so they resemble spokes of a wheel. Place strips on the bottom and up the sides of a 3-qt. slow cooker. Coat strips with cooking spray.
2. In a large bowl, combine the bread crumbs, 1 cup spaghetti sauce, egg, onion, and seasonings. Crumble beef over mixture and mix well. Shape into a loaf; place in the center of the strips.
3. Spoon remaining spaghetti sauce over meat loaf. Cover and cook on low for 3-4 hours or until a thermometer reads 160°. Using foil strips as handles, remove meat loaf to a platter.

> ❝What could be easier than an Italian-inspired meat loaf made in the slow cooker? No fuss, easy cleanup and great homemade flavor; it's all right here!❞
> — **SHARON DELANEY-CHRONIS** SOUTH MILWAUKEE, WISCONSIN

Beef Vegetable Soup

Convenient frozen veggies and hash browns make this meaty soup a snap to mix up. Simply brown the ground beef, then stir everything together to simmer all day. It's wonderful served with bread and a salad.
— **CAROL CALHOUN** SIOUX FALLS, SOUTH DAKOTA

PREP: 10 MIN. **COOK:** 8 HOURS **MAKES:** 10 SERVINGS (2½ QUARTS)

- 1 pound ground beef
- 1 can (46 ounces) tomato juice
- 1 package (16 ounces) frozen mixed vegetables, thawed
- 2 cups frozen cubed hash brown potatoes, thawed
- 1 envelope onion soup mix

1. In a large skillet, cook beef over medium heat until no longer pink; drain. Transfer to a 5-qt. slow cooker. Stir in the tomato juice, mixed vegetables, potatoes and soup mix.
2. Cover and cook on low for 8-10 hours or until heated through.

Two-Step Stroganoff

I especially like to use my slow cooker on hot summer days when I want to keep my kitchen cool. I'm always trying new recipes for different functions, but Stroganoff is a favorite I turn to again and again.
— **ROBERTA MENEFEE** WALCOTT, NEW YORK

PREP: 15 MIN. **COOK:** 7 HOURS **MAKES:** 6 SERVINGS

- 2 pounds ground beef, cooked and drained
- 2 medium onions, chopped
- 1 cup beef consomme
- 1 can (4 ounces) mushroom stems and pieces, drained
- 3 tablespoons tomato paste
- 2 garlic cloves, minced
- 1½ teaspoons salt
- ¼ teaspoon pepper
- 2 tablespoons all-purpose flour
- ¾ cup sour cream
  Hot cooked egg noodles

In a 3-qt. slow cooker, combine the first eight ingredients. Cover and cook on low for 6 hours. In a small bowl, combine flour and sour cream until smooth; stir into beef mixture. Cover and cook 1 hour longer or until thickened. Serve over noodles.

Cooking the stuffed peppers in a slow cooker is not only convenient, but the long cooking process makes the meaty filling even more flavorful.

— TASTE OF HOME TEST KITCHEN

ITALIAN STUFFED PEPPERS

Italian Stuffed Peppers

PREP: 25 MIN. **COOK:** 4 HOURS
MAKES: 6 SERVINGS

- 6 large green or sweet red peppers
- 1 pound lean ground beef (90% lean)
- 2 cups cubed part-skim mozzarella cheese (¼-inch cubes)
- 1 cup uncooked converted rice
- 1 small onion, chopped
- 2 garlic cloves, minced
- 1 teaspoon minced fresh parsley
- 1 teaspoon salt
- ½ teaspoon pepper
- 1 can (28 ounces) crushed tomatoes
- 1 cup beef broth
- ½ cup grated Parmesan cheese
  Additional minced fresh parsley

1. Cut tops off peppers and remove seeds; set aside. In a large bowl, combine the beef, mozzarella cheese, rice, onion, garlic, parsley, salt and pepper; spoon into peppers. Transfer to an oval 5- or 6-qt. slow cooker. Pour tomatoes over peppers; pour broth around the sides.

2. Cover and cook on low for 4-5 hours or until a thermometer reads 160° and peppers are tender. Sprinkle with Parmesan cheese and additional parsley.

Cranberry Meatballs

Whether you serve them as appetizers or the main course, these tasty meatballs are sure to be popular. The sweet and tangy sauce makes them irresistible.

— **NINA HALL** SPOKANE, WASHINGTON

PREP: 20 MIN. **COOK:** 6 HOURS
MAKES: 6 SERVINGS

- 2 eggs, beaten
- 1 cup dry bread crumbs
- ⅓ cup minced fresh parsley
- 2 tablespoons finely chopped onion
- 1½ pounds lean ground beef (90% lean)
- 1 can (14 ounces) jellied cranberry sauce
- 1 bottle (12 ounces) chili sauce
- ⅓ cup ketchup
- 2 tablespoons brown sugar
- 1 tablespoon lemon juice

1. In a large bowl, combine the eggs, bread crumbs, parsley and onion. Crumble beef over mixture and mix well. Shape into 1½-in. balls. Place in a 3-qt. slow cooker.

2. In another bowl, combine the cranberry sauce, chili sauce, ketchup, brown sugar and lemon juice. Pour over meatballs. Cover and cook on low for 6-7 hours or until meat is no longer pink.

Meat Loaf Burgers

PREP: 15 MIN. **COOK:** 7 HOURS
MAKES: 6 SERVINGS

- 1 **large onion, sliced**
- 1 **celery rib, chopped**
- 2 **pounds lean ground beef (90% lean)**
- 1½ **teaspoons salt, divided**
- ¼ **teaspoon pepper**
- 2 **cups tomato juice**
- 4 **garlic cloves, minced**
- 1 **tablespoon ketchup**
- 1 **teaspoon Italian seasoning**
- 1 **bay leaf**
- 6 **hamburger buns, split**

1. Place onion and celery in a 3-qt. slow cooker. Combine beef, 1 teaspoon salt and pepper; shape into six patties. Place over onion mixture. Combine the tomato juice, garlic, ketchup, Italian seasoning, bay leaf and remaining salt. Pour over patties.

2. Cover and cook on low for 7-9 hours or until meat is no longer pink. Discard bay leaf. Separate patties with a spatula if necessary; serve on buns.

Slow Cooker Cheese Dip

I brought this slightly spicy cheese dip to a gathering with friends and it was a huge hit. The spicy pork sausage provides the zip!

— **MARION BARTONE** CONNEAUT, OHIO

PREP: 15 MIN. **COOK:** 4 HOURS
MAKES: 2 QUARTS

- 1 **pound ground beef**
- ½ **pound bulk spicy pork sausage**
- 2 **pounds process cheese (Velveeta), cubed**
- 2 **cans (10 ounces each) diced tomatoes and green chilies**
  Tortilla chips

1. In a large skillet, cook beef and sausage over medium heat until no longer pink; drain. Transfer to a 3- or 4-qt. slow cooker. Stir in cheese and tomatoes.

2. Cover and cook on low for 4-5 hours or until cheese is melted, stirring occasionally. Serve with chips.

These hearty sandwiches are perfect for potlucks. Served on hamburger buns, the patties get extra flavor when topped with the seasoned tomato sauce.

— **PEGGY BURDICK** BURLINGTON, MICHIGAN

MEAT LOAF BURGERS

104

100

107

Sides
& More

Western-Style Beef and Beans

PREP: 15 MIN. **BAKE:** 1 HOUR
MAKES: 12 SERVINGS

- 3 pounds ground beef
- 2 medium onions, chopped
- 2 celery ribs, chopped
- 2 teaspoons beef bouillon granules
- ⅔ cup boiling water
- 2 cans (28 ounces each) baked beans with molasses
- 1½ cups ketchup
- ¼ cup prepared mustard
- 3 garlic cloves, minced
- 1½ teaspoons salt
- ½ teaspoon pepper
- ½ pound sliced bacon, cooked and crumbled

1. In a Dutch oven over medium heat, cook the beef, onions and celery until meat is no longer pink; drain. Dissolve bouillon in water; stir into beef mixture. Add the beans, ketchup, mustard, garlic, salt and pepper; mix well.

2. Transfer to an ungreased 3-qt. baking dish. Cover and bake at 375° for 60-70 minutes or until bubbly; stir. Sprinkle with bacon.

Hearty Spinach Salad

Ground beef turns spinach salad into a hearty and satisfying dish. You can easily substitute any type of lettuce for the spinach.

— **RITA GOSHAW**
SOUTH MILWAUKEE, WISCONSIN

PREP/TOTAL TIME: 20 MIN.
MAKES: 8 SERVINGS

- 1 pound ground beef
- 6 garlic cloves, minced
- 1 package (10 ounces) fresh spinach, torn
- 2 large tomatoes, cut into wedges
- 2 cups (4 ounces each) shredded cheddar cheese
- ½ cup sliced fresh mushrooms
  Salt and pepper to taste
  Salad dressing of your choice

1. In a large skillet, cook beef and garlic over medium heat until the meat is no longer pink; drain.

2. In a salad bowl, combine the spinach, beef, tomatoes, cheese, mushrooms, salt and pepper. Drizzle with salad dressing; toss to coat.

This crowd-pleasing side dish doesn't take long to make but tastes like it simmered all day. You can also serve it as an entree with bread and a salad.

— **JOLENE LOPEZ** WICHITA, KANSAS

WESTERN-STYLE BEEF AND BEANS

Spicy Beef Salad

Here's a delectable salad that doesn't skimp on flavor. I make it often, especially on days when I'm pressed for time. My husband, my mother and I all give it thumbs-up!

— **NATERCIA YAILAIAN**
SOMERVILLE, MASSACHUSETTS

PREP/TOTAL TIME: 25 MIN.
MAKES: 8 SERVINGS

- 1 **pound ground beef**
- ⅓ **cup canola oil**
- 3 **tablespoons lime juice**
- 2 **tablespoons soy sauce**
- 2 **tablespoons molasses**
- 1 **small jalapeno pepper, seeded and minced**
- 1 **garlic clove, minced**
- ¾ **teaspoon ground ginger**
- 6 **cups torn salad greens**
- 1 **large tomato, cut into wedges**
- 2 **green onions, sliced**
  Jalapeno pepper and lime slices, optional

1. In a large skillet, cook beef over medium heat until no longer pink; drain.
2. Meanwhile, in a small bowl, combine the oil, lime juice, soy sauce, molasses, jalapeno, garlic and ginger.
3. Stir into the beef. Cook and stir until heated through.
4. On a large serving platter, layer the salad greens, tomato, beef mixture and green onions.
5. Garnish the salad with thinly sliced jalapeno pepper and lime if desired.

Editor's Note: *Wear disposable gloves when cutting hot peppers; the oils can burn skin. Avoid touching your face.*

Pizza Loaf

Grandma made her yummy pizza loaf often when I was growing up and it was always a favorite of mine. Now it's a favorite of my husband and two kids!

— **AMANDA WIERSEMA** ARCHER, IOWA

PREP: 25 MIN. **BAKE:** 20 MIN. **MAKES:** 6 SERVINGS

- 1 **pound ground beef**
- ½ **cup chopped onion**
- ½ **cup chopped green pepper**
- 1 **cup Italian tomato sauce**
- 1 **can (4 ounces) mushroom stems and pieces, drained**
- 1 **teaspoon paprika**
- ½ **teaspoon garlic salt**
- ½ **teaspoon dried oregano**
- ⅛ **teaspoon pepper**
- 1 **tube (13.8 ounces) refrigerated pizza crust**
- ½ **cup shredded part-skim mozzarella cheese**
- ½ **cup shredded cheddar cheese**

1. In a large skillet, cook the beef, onion and green pepper over medium heat until meat is no longer pink; drain. Stir in the tomato sauce, mushrooms and seasonings.
2. Unroll pizza dough onto a greased baking sheet; roll into a 15-in. x 12-in. rectangle. Spoon meat mixture down center of rectangle; sprinkle with cheeses.
3. On each long side, cut 1-in.-wide strips about 2½ in. into center. Starting at one end, fold alternating strips at an angle across filling. Pinch ends to seal.
4. Bake at 350° for 20-25 minutes or until golden brown.

2. In a large skillet, cook beef and onion over medium heat until meat is no longer pink; drain. Add the ketchup, mustard and pepper; heat through.

3. Divide lettuce among four dinner plates; top each with tomatoes, meat mixture, cheese and bacon. Garnish with croutons and pickles.

Stuffed Tomatoes

I learned to put an Italian twist on my cooking after I married my husband, who is of Italian descent. I like to prepare these tomatoes for company.

— **MARION AMONTE** HINGHAM, MASSACHUSETTS

PREP: 30 MIN. **BAKE:** 35 MIN. **MAKES:** 6 SERVINGS

6	**large tomatoes**
1	**pound ground beef**
1	**cup cooked long grain rice**
2	**tablespoons minced fresh parsley**
1	**teaspoon dried basil**
1	**teaspoon salt**
1	**teaspoon pepper**
½	**cup grated Parmesan cheese**
¼	**pound Swiss cheese, cut into ½-inch cubes**

1. Cut a thin slice off the top of each tomato and discard; remove the cores. Carefully scoop out and reserve pulp, leaving ½-in. shells. Invert tomatoes onto paper towels to drain. Chop the reserved pulp.

2. In a large skillet, cook beef until no longer pink; drain. Add the rice, parsley, basil, salt, pepper and tomato pulp; heat through. Remove from the heat; stir in cheeses.

3. Spoon filling into tomato shells. Place in a greased shallow baking dish. Bake, uncovered, at 350° for 35 minutes or until heated through.

Bacon Cheeseburger Salad

Think your kids won't eat salad? Try our cheeseburger salad and see what happens! Cooked ground beef is mixed with ketchup and mustard, then placed on lettuce and served with all of their favorite burger toppings.

— **TASTE OF HOME TEST KITCHEN**

PREP/TOTAL TIME: 30 MIN. **MAKES:** 4 SERVINGS

2	**hamburger buns, cut into 1-inch cubes**
2	**teaspoons olive oil**
⅛	**teaspoon garlic salt**
1	**pound ground beef**
¾	**cup chopped onion**
¾	**cup ketchup**
1	**tablespoon prepared mustard**
⅛	**teaspoon pepper**
8	**cups shredded lettuce**
2	**cups chopped tomatoes**
4	**slices process American cheese, cut into strips**
½	**cup crumbled cooked bacon**
8	**dill pickle slices**

1. For croutons, place bun cubes on a baking sheet. Drizzle with oil and sprinkle with garlic salt; toss to coat. Broil 4 in. from the heat for 4-6 minutes or until golden brown, turning once. Set aside.

Cherry Baked Beans

PREP: 20 MIN. **BAKE:** 40 MIN. **MAKES:** 12 SERVINGS

- 1 pound lean ground beef (90% lean)
- 2 cans (15 ounces each) pork and beans
- 2 cups frozen pitted tart cherries, thawed
- 1 can (16 ounces) kidney beans, rinsed and drained
- 1 cup ketchup
- ½ cup water
- 1 envelope onion soup mix
- 2 tablespoons prepared mustard
- 2 teaspoons cider vinegar

1. In a large skillet, cook beef over medium heat until no longer pink; drain. In a large bowl, combine the remaining ingredients; stir in beef.

2. Transfer to an ungreased 2½ qt. baking dish. Bake, uncovered, at 400° for 40-45 minutes or until heated through, stirring occasionally.

66 Here's a perfect dish to bring to a family reunion or any get-together. It's fast and easy to prepare, and you won't ever have to worry about taking home leftovers...because there won't be any! 99

— **MARGARET SMITH** SUPERIOR, WISCONSIN

Potluck Mushroom Rice

We hold potluck dinners once a week at work. A co-worker brought this excellent dish, and I left with the recipe. It's versatile because you can add different seasonings to suit your tastes.

— **YVONNE TAYLOR** ROBSTOWN, TEXAS

PREP: 30 MIN. **COOK:** 30 MIN. **MAKES:** 12-14 SERVINGS

- 3 cups water
- 1½ teaspoons beef bouillon granules
- 1½ cups uncooked long grain rice
- 2 pounds ground beef
- 1 large onion, chopped
- 1 large green pepper, chopped
- 1 jar (6 ounces) whole mushrooms, drained
- 1 can (4 ounces) mushroom stems and pieces, drained
- 1 celery rib, sliced
- 1 can (10¾ ounces) condensed cream of celery soup, undiluted
- 1 can (10¾ ounces) condensed cream of mushroom soup, undiluted
- 2 tablespoons Worcestershire sauce
- ½ teaspoon garlic powder

1. In a saucepan, bring water and bouillon to a boil. Stir in rice. Reduce heat; cover and simmer for 15-20 minutes or until tender.

2. In a large skillet, cook the beef, onion, green pepper, mushrooms and celery until meat is no longer pink; drain. Stir in the soups, Worcestershire sauce, garlic powder and cooked rice.

3. Transfer to a greased 3-qt. baking dish (dish will be full). Cover and bake at 350° for 30 minutes or until heated through.

Gyro Salad with Tzatziki Dressing

PREP/TOTAL TIME: 30 MIN.
MAKES: 4-6 SERVINGS

DRESSING

- 1 cucumber, peeled and coarsely shredded
- ½ teaspoon salt
- ½ cup sour cream
- ¾ cup (6 ounces) plain yogurt
- 2 tablespoons white vinegar
- 1 garlic clove, minced
- ½ teaspoon dill weed
- ¼ teaspoon cracked black pepper

SALAD

- ½ pound ground beef or lamb
- 1 small onion, chopped
- 1 teaspoon Greek seasoning or oregano
- 1 package (10 ounces) romaine salad blend
- 2 tomatoes, chopped
- 1 package (4 ounces) crumbled feta cheese
- ½ cup pitted Greek olives, drained
  Toasted pita bread wedges

1. In a large bowl, sprinkle cucumber with salt; mix well. Let stand for 5 minutes. Drain. Stir in remaining dressing ingredients. Refrigerate until serving.
2. In a large skillet over medium heat, cook beef, onion and Greek seasoning until meat is no longer pink; drain.
3. Arrange salad blend on a large serving platter; top with tomatoes, cheese, olives and beef. Spoon dressing over the top. Serve immediately with pita wedges.

Black Bean Taco Salad

Here's a delicious entree salad that will please even your pickiest eaters. The flavors are mild and pleasant.

— TASTE OF HOME TEST KITCHEN

PREP/TOTAL TIME: 20 MIN.
MAKES: 4 SERVINGS

- 1 pound ground beef
- 4 cups torn leaf lettuce
- 1 large tomato, chopped
- 1 cup canned black beans, rinsed and drained
- ½ cup Catalina salad dressing
- 4 cups nacho-flavored tortilla chips

1. In a large skillet, cook beef over medium heat until no longer pink; drain. In a large bowl, combine the lettuce, tomato, beans and beef. Drizzle with dressing and toss to coat.
2. Arrange tortilla chips on a serving plate; top with beef mixture.

If you're fond of gyros, you'll enjoy our garden-fresh salad that showcases flavorful meat and delectable Greek ingredients.

— TASTE OF HOME COOKING SCHOOL

GYRO SALAD WITH TZATZIKI DRESSING

SIDES & MORE

Italian Spinach Braid

I've been making this nutritious bread for more than 25 years. It's how I got my kids to eat spinach when they were little.

— **PAT JASPER** NORTHLAKE, ILLINOIS

PREP: 20 MIN. + RISING
BAKE: 20 MIN. **MAKES:** 6 SERVINGS

- 1 loaf (1 pound) frozen whole wheat bread dough, thawed
- 1 pound lean ground beef (90% lean)
- 1 package (10 ounces) frozen chopped spinach, thawed and squeezed dry
- ⅔ cup shredded part-skim mozzarella cheese
- 2 tablespoons grated Romano cheese
- ¾ teaspoon dried minced garlic
- ¾ teaspoon fennel seed
- ¾ teaspoon dried oregano
- ½ teaspoon salt
- 1 egg white, beaten
  Pizza sauce, optional

1. Roll dough into a 12-in. x 9-in. rectangle. Transfer to a 15-in. x 10-in. x 1-in. baking pan coated with cooking spray. Cover and let rise in a warm place until doubled, about 1 hour.
2. Meanwhile, in a large skillet, cook beef over medium heat until no longer pink; drain. Transfer to a large bowl; add the spinach, cheeses, garlic, fennel seed, oregano and salt.
3. Spread beef mixture lengthwise down the center of dough. On each long side, cut 1-in.-wide strips 3 in. into center.
4. Starting at one end, fold alternating strips at an angle across filling. Pinch ends to seal. Brush with egg white. Bake at 350° for 20-25 minutes or until golden brown. Serve with pizza sauce if desired.

Portuguese Dressing

PREP: 20 MIN. **BAKE:** 55 MIN. **MAKES:** 8 SERVINGS

- 1 pound ground beef
- 1 medium onion, chopped
- ½ pound smoked sausage, chopped
- 2 teaspoons poultry seasoning
- ½ teaspoon garlic powder
- ⅛ teaspoon ground allspice
- 1 package (12 ounces) unseasoned stuffing cubes
- 1 can (14½ ounces) chicken broth
- 1 egg, lightly beaten
- ¼ cup minced fresh parsley
- 2 tablespoons butter, melted

1. In a large skillet, cook beef and onion over medium heat until meat is no longer pink; drain. Transfer to a large bowl. In the same skillet, saute the sausage, poultry seasoning, garlic powder and allspice for 2 minutes.
2. Add the sausage mixture, stuffing cubes, broth, egg and parsley to the beef mixture; mix well. Transfer to a greased 3-qt. baking dish. Drizzle with butter.
3. Cover and bake at 325° for 45 minutes. Uncover; bake 10-15 minutes longer or until lightly browned and a thermometer reads 160°.

  “With beef and smoked sausage, this meaty side dish is different from many other dressing and stuffing recipes. It's perfect for special occasions with roasted chicken or turkey.”

— **JEAN REPOSE** NORTH KINGSTOWN, RHODE ISLAND

Poppy Seed Squares

When I came across these unusual pastries, I just knew I had to try them. Although I prepare the tender squares every Christmas, no one tires of them.

— **JO BADEN** INDEPENDENCE, KANSAS

PREP: 35 MIN. **BAKE:** 25 MIN. **MAKES:** ABOUT 10 DOZEN

- 1 **pound ground beef**
- 1½ **cups finely chopped fresh mushrooms**
- 1 **medium onion, finely chopped**
- 1 **can (10¾ ounces) condensed cream of celery or mushroom soup, undiluted**
- 1 **tablespoon prepared horseradish**
- 1 **teaspoon salt**
- ½ **teaspoon pepper**

CRUST
- 3 **cups all-purpose flour**
- 2 **tablespoons poppy seeds**
- ¾ **teaspoon baking powder**
- ¾ **teaspoon salt**
- 1 **cup shortening**
- ½ **cup cold water**

1. In a large skillet, cook the beef, mushrooms and onion over medium heat until meat is no longer pink. Add the soup, horseradish, salt and pepper. Remove from the heat; set aside.
2. In a large bowl, combine the flour, poppy seeds, baking powder and salt. Cut in shortening until the mixture resembles coarse crumbs. Gradually add water, tossing with a fork until a ball forms. Divide dough in half. Roll out one portion into a 15-in. x 10-in. rectangle; transfer to an ungreased 15-in. x 10-in. x 1-in. baking pan.
3. Spoon meat mixture over dough. Roll out the remaining dough into 15-in. x 10-in. rectangle; place over filling. Bake at 425° for 25 minutes or until golden brown. Cut into small squares.

Beef-Stuffed Crescents

PREP: 30 MIN. **BAKE:** 15 MIN. **MAKES:** 32 APPETIZERS

- ¾ **pound ground beef**
- ¼ **cup chopped onion**
- 2 **garlic cloves, minced**
- 1 **cup (4 ounces) shredded cheddar cheese**
- 1 **tablespoon sweet pickle relish**
- ½ **teaspoon salt**
- ½ **teaspoon chili powder**
- ¼ **teaspoon pepper**
   Dash sugar
- 2 **tubes (8 ounces each) refrigerated crescent rolls**

1. In a large skillet, cook beef, onion and garlic over medium heat until meat is no longer pink; drain. Stir in the cheese, pickle relish, salt, chili powder, pepper and sugar; set aside.
2. Unroll crescent dough and separate into triangles. Cut each in half lengthwise, forming two triangles. Place 1 tablespoon beef mixture along the wide end of each triangle; gently roll up.
3. Place rolls point side down 2 in. apart on ungreased baking sheets. Bake at 375° for 11-15 minutes or until golden brown. Serve warm.

❝My family loves these hearty appetizers throughout the year. They are nice for munching or alongside soup. Pickle relish adds the perfect hint of sweetness. ❞
— **ALENE KNESEL** NORTHOME, MINNESOTA

SIDES & MORE

Crowd-Pleasing Taco Salad

PREP/TOTAL TIME: 30 MIN.
MAKES: 10 SERVINGS

- 1 **pound ground beef**
- ½ **cup ketchup**
- 1 **teaspoon dried oregano**
- 1 **teaspoon chili powder**
- ½ **teaspoon salt**
- ¼ **teaspoon pepper**
- 1 **medium head iceberg lettuce, torn**
- 2 **medium tomatoes, diced**
- 1 **cup (4 ounces) shredded Mexican cheese blend**
- 1 **can (2¼ ounces) sliced ripe olives, drained**
- ½ **cup mayonnaise**
- ¼ **cup taco sauce**
- 1 **package (10½ ounces) corn chips**

1. In a large saucepan, cook beef over medium heat until no longer pink; drain. Stir in the ketchup, oregano, chili powder, salt and pepper. Bring to a boil. Reduce heat; cover and simmer for 10 minutes.
2. In a large bowl, combine the lettuce, tomatoes, cheese, olives and beef mixture. Combine mayonnaise and taco sauce; pour over salad and toss to coat. Sprinkle with corn chips. Serve immediately.

Cheesy Broccoli Rice

Looking for a new side dish for your holiday dinners? Try this delicious recipe that combines tender rice, nutritious broccoli and savory cheese!

— **KAREN WEAVILL**
JOHNSTON, RHODE ISLAND

PREP: 15 MIN. **BAKE:** 30 MIN.
MAKES: 6 SERVINGS

- 1 **pound ground beef**
- 1 **medium onion, diced**
- 1 **garlic clove, minced**
- 3 **cups cooked long grain rice**
- 2 **cups fresh or frozen chopped broccoli, thawed**
- 2 **cups (8 ounces) shredded cheddar cheese**
- 2 **tablespoon grated Parmesan cheese**

1. In a skillet, cook beef, onion and garlic over medium heat until the meat is no longer pink; drain. Stir in the rice, broccoli and cheddar cheese.
2. Transfer to a greased 13-in. x 9-in. baking dish. Sprinkle with Parmesan cheese. Bake, uncovered, at 350° for 30-40 minutes or until heated through.

CROWD-PLEASING TACO SALAD

General Index

ALPHABETICAL INDEX